TypeScript for JavaScript Developers

The Essential Guide for JavaScript Developers to
Write Safer, Scalable, and More Efficient Code

Adriam Miller

DISCOVER OTHER BOOKS IN THE SERIES.. 4

DISCLAIMER 6

INTRODUCTION 7

CHAPTER 1: INTRODUCTION TYPESCRIPT FOR JAVASCRIPT
DEVELOPERS... 9

THE POWER OF TYPESCRIPT FOR JAVASCRIPT DEVELOPERS 12
TYPESCRIPT FOR JAVASCRIPT FUNDAMENTALS.. 16

CHAPTER 2: GETTING STARTED WITH TYPESCRIPT FOR
JAVASCRIPT... 22

INSTALLING AND SETTING UP TYPESCRIPT IN YOUR PROJECT 27
UNDERSTANDING TSCONFIG.JSON AND COMPILER OPTIONS................................. 32

CHAPTER 3: TYPESCRIPT'S POWERFUL TYPE SYSTEM................ 37

PRIMITIVE AND COMPLEX TYPES (STRING, NUMBER, BOOLEAN, OBJECT, ANY,
NEVER, UNKNOWN) 41
TYPE INFERENCE VS EXPLICIT TYPING... 45

CHAPTER 4: MASTERING FUNCTIONS IN TYPESCRIPT................ 51

STRONGLY TYPED FUNCTION PARAMETERS AND RETURN TYPES........................... 57
FUNCTION OVERLOADING AND ADVANCED TYPING IN FUNCTIONS........................ 61

CHAPTER 5: WORKING WITH OBJECTS AND INTERFACES......... 67

DEFINING AND EXTENDING INTERFACES FOR CLEANER CODE............................... 71
USING TYPE ALIASES AND INTERSECTION TYPES FOR FLEXIBILITY 75

CHAPTER 6: ADVANCED TYPESCRIPT FEATURES FOR
SCALABLE CODE.. 80

WORKING WITH UNION AND LITERAL TYPES FOR SAFER CODE 85
MAPPED AND CONDITIONAL TYPES FOR ADVANCED TYPE MANIPULATION 90

CHAPTER 7: OBJECT-ORIENTED PROGRAMMING IN
TYPESCRIPT 96

CLASSES, INHERITANCE, AND ACCESS MODIFIERS (PUBLIC, PRIVATE, PROTECTED)
.... 102
ABSTRACT CLASSES VS INTERFACES 108

CHAPTER 8: HANDLING ARRAYS, TUPLES, AND ENUMS
EFFECTIVELY.. 113

TYPED ARRAYS AND TUPLES FOR MORE PREDICTABLE DATA STRUCTURES 119

LEVERAGING ENUMS TO WRITE MORE READABLE CODE 124

CHAPTER 9: MASTERING TYPE GUARDS AND ADVANCED TYPE SAFETY 130

USING TYPEOF, INSTANCEOF, AND CUSTOM TYPE GUARDS 135

HANDLING UNKNOWN AND OPTIONAL VALUES WITH UNKNOWN AND OPTIONAL CHAINING 140

CHAPTER 10: WORKING WITH MODULES AND NAMESPACES. 146

ES6 MODULES AND TYPESCRIPT—HOW TO STRUCTURE YOUR CODEBASE 150

LEVERAGING TYPESCRIPT DECLARATION FILES (.D.TS) FOR THIRD-PARTY LIBRARIES 156

CHAPTER 11: ERROR HANDLING AND DEBUGGING IN TYPESCRIPT 160

COMMON TYPESCRIPT ERRORS AND HOW TO FIX THEM 166

DEBUGGING TYPESCRIPT CODE WITH VS CODE AND DEVELOPER TOOLS 172

CONCLUSION 177

BIOGRAPHY 178

GLOSSARY: TYPESCRIPT FOR JAVASCRIPT DEVELOPERS 179

Discover Other Books in the Series

"TypeScript for Beginners: A Beginner's Guide to the Future of JavaScript"

"TypeScript for Backend Development: Backend applications with Node.js, Express, and modern frameworks"

"TypeScript for Blockchain: Unlock the full potential of TypeScript in Web3 development"

"TypeScript for DevOps: The Secret Weapon for Automating, Scaling, and Securing Your Infrastructure"

"Typescript for Front End Development: Reduce Errors, Boost Productivity, and Master Modern Web Development Like a Pro"

"Typescript for Microservices: Learn How to Leverage TypeScript to Develop Robust, Maintainable, and Efficient Microservices Architecture"

"TypeScript for Mobile Application Development: Build Faster, Safer, and Smarter Applications with Ease"

"TypeScript for Web Development: Boost Your Productivity, Eliminate Costly Errors, and Build Scalable Web Applications with TypeScript"

Disclaimer

The information provided in this book, **"TypeScript for JavaScript Developers: The Essential Guide for JavaScript Developers to Write Safer, Scalable, and More Efficient Code"** by Adrian Miller, is for **educational and informational purposes only**. The content is designed to help readers understand TypeScript programming.

Introduction

Welcome to "**TypeScript for JavaScript Developers: The Essential Guide for JavaScript Developers to Write Safer, Scalable, and More Efficient Code.**" As the field of web development progresses, the necessity for more robust, maintainable, and efficient coding practices has reached unprecedented levels. This book is tailored specifically for JavaScript developers who aspire to elevate their expertise by integrating TypeScript into their development processes.

JavaScript stands as a highly adaptable and extensively utilized programming language that has fueled a multitude of applications and frameworks, establishing itself as a cornerstone of contemporary web development. Nevertheless, as applications become increasingly intricate, the dynamic characteristics of JavaScript can present challenges, including runtime errors, code that lacks clarity, and the growing difficulty of managing extensive codebases. This is where TypeScript proves invaluable.

TypeScript serves as a superset of JavaScript, introducing static typing that enables developers to identify errors during compilation rather than at runtime. By offering type definitions, interfaces, and various advanced features, TypeScript equips developers to produce code that is not only more comprehensible but also safer and more scalable. In this guide, we will examine how adopting TypeScript can enhance your development experience and elevate the quality of your code.

Within this book, you will discover practical guidance, straightforward examples, and interactive exercises aimed at bridging the gap between your current JavaScript expertise and the TypeScript environment. We will delve into the essential concepts of TypeScript, including types, interfaces, generics, and decorators, as well as best practices for incorporating TypeScript into your projects, whether you are developing small applications or large-scale systems.

You will also discover how TypeScript fits into popular frameworks and libraries such as React, Angular, and Node.js, as well as how to leverage existing JavaScript libraries within a TypeScript project. By the end of this book, you will be equipped with the knowledge and confidence to write safer, more efficient code that stands the test of time.

Whether you're a seasoned JavaScript developer aiming to improve your skills or a newcomer looking to build a strong foundation in TypeScript, this guide will serve as your essential resource. Let's embark on this journey together and unlock the full potential of TypeScript, making your code not only functional but also a joy to work with. Welcome to the world of TypeScript!

Chapter 1: Introduction TypeScript for JavaScript Developers

TypeScript is a superset of JavaScript that introduces static typing and various advanced features to improve the development process.

Understanding TypeScript

TypeScript is an open-source programming language created by Microsoft, first released in 2012 to address significant challenges encountered by JavaScript developers. As a superset of JavaScript, it ensures that any valid JavaScript code is also valid in TypeScript. This compatibility facilitates a gradual integration of TypeScript into existing projects, allowing developers to leverage the advantages of type safety and contemporary language features without necessitating a complete overhaul of their codebase.

The primary feature that sets TypeScript apart is its static typing system. In contrast to JavaScript's dynamic typing, TypeScript allows developers to define data types for variables, function parameters, and return values. This capability enables the identification of type-related errors during the compilation process rather than at runtime, which can lead to critical failures in production environments. By utilizing TypeScript, developers can explicitly declare types, resulting in improved documentation, better tooling support, and enhanced maintainability of the code.## Why TypeScript?

1. Enhanced Code Quality and Maintainability

As JavaScript applications scale, maintaining the code quality can become challenging. TypeScript's static typing system provides developers with the tools to define contracts for their code. By explicitly specifying types, developers can ensure that functions receive the correct inputs and return the expected outputs, reducing the risk of runtime errors.

2. Improved Developer Experience

TypeScript comes with excellent tooling support, including autocompletion, easier refactoring, and more relevant compiler messages. Modern IDEs and text editors can leverage TypeScript's type information to provide developers with features like real-time error detection and code navigation, greatly enhancing productivity.

3. Modern Language Features

TypeScript embraces many features from modern JavaScript standards (ES6 and beyond), such as arrow functions, destructuring, spread syntax, async/await, and more. Additionally, TypeScript introduces features such as interfaces, enums, tuple types, and generics, making it easier to model complex data structures and patterns.

4. Compatibility with JavaScript Ecosystem

Since TypeScript is a superset of JavaScript, you can leverage existing JavaScript libraries and frameworks without any issue. Popular frameworks like React, Angular, and Vue have embraced TypeScript, providing first-class support and allowing developers to write more robust and type-safe applications.

Getting Started with TypeScript

As a JavaScript developer, transitioning to TypeScript does not require a complete overhaul of your existing knowledge. Familiar concepts, such as variables, functions, and objects, remain relevant, while you will gain new skills to manage types and interfaces effectively.

To start using TypeScript, you can follow these simple steps:

Installation: Install TypeScript globally using npm with the command `npm install -g typescript`. You can also set it up for a specific project using `npm install --save-dev typescript`.

Configuration: Create a `tsconfig.json` file in your project directory. This file allows you to specify compiler options and the files you want TypeScript to include in the compilation process.

Writing TypeScript: Start by renaming your JavaScript files from `.js` to `.ts`. You can gradually introduce type annotations and other TypeScript features in your code.

Compiling TypeScript: Use the TypeScript compiler (`tsc`) to transpile your TypeScript code into JavaScript. This step prepares your code for deployment in any environment that runs JavaScript.

By embracing TypeScript, developers can enjoy a richer tooling ecosystem and mitigate some of the common pitfalls of dynamic typing. In the chapters that follow, we will delve deeper into TypeScript's various features, best practices, and how to integrate it into both new and existing projects seamlessly. Whether you are building a small application or a large-scale enterprise solution, TypeScript stands out as an invaluable ally in the world of modern web development.

The Power of Typescript for JavaScript Developers

In this chapter, we will explore the transformative power of TypeScript for JavaScript developers, highlighting its features, benefits, and practical implementation strategies.

1. Understanding TypeScript

TypeScript was created by Microsoft in 2012 to address some of the challenges posed by JavaScript, especially in large-scale applications. At its core, TypeScript is JavaScript with type annotations. This means that while all valid JavaScript code is also valid TypeScript code, TypeScript extends JavaScript's capabilities by introducing a type system and additional features such as interfaces, enums, and more.

1.1. Strong Typing

One of TypeScript's standout features is its strong typing, which helps developers catch errors at compile time rather than at runtime. By specifying types for variables, function parameters, and return values, developers can create more predictable and robust code. For example:

```typescript
function greet(name: string): string { return `Hello, ${name}!`;
}
let user = greet("Alice"); // Correct usage
let error = greet(42); // Compile-time error: Argument of type 'number' is not assignable to parameter of type
```

'string'.
```
```

This early detection of type errors minimizes debugging time and leads to a smoother development experience.

1.2. Enhanced Code Readability and Maintainability

TypeScript promotes better documentation within the code itself. With explicit type annotations and interfaces, developers can quickly understand what data structures should look like, making it easier to navigate and maintain code. As an added bonus, TypeScript's infrastructure facilitates documentation generation, enabling teams to produce high-quality documentation seamlessly.

2. Tooling and Integration

TypeScript is designed to work well with existing JavaScript tools and libraries, ensuring a smooth integration process. Popular development environments such as Visual Studio Code provide extensive support for TypeScript, with features like IntelliSense, autocompletion, and debugging enhancements. These tools help developers write code more efficiently and reduce the chances of errors.

2.1. IDE Support

Incorporating TypeScript into your development workflow brings significant benefits through integration with various integrated development environments (IDEs). Today's popular IDEs, such as Visual Studio Code, WebStorm, and Atom, provide features like:

Real-time feedback: As you type, the IDE will highlight errors, warnings, and suggestions.

Refactoring tools: Developers can easily rename variables, extract methods, and perform other refactoring tasks.

Type assertions and inference: The IDE assists in inferring types, reducing the need for explicit annotations while still benefiting from TypeScript's type safety.

3. TypeScript Features for Advanced Development

Beyond basic type annotations, TypeScript boasts a wealth of advanced features that enhance development capabilities.

3.1. Interfaces and Type Aliases

Interfaces and type aliases allow developers to create complex data types and enforce structure across their applications. This is particularly helpful in large teams, where collaboration might lead to inconsistencies without a well-defined structure.

```typescript
interface User {
id: number; name: string; email: string;
}
const user: User = { id: 1,
name: "Alice",
email: "alice@example.com",
};
```

3.2. Generics

Generics enable the creation of reusable components that

work with various data types while maintaining type safety. This flexibility is helpful for building libraries or applications that require high modularity.

```typescript
function identity<T>(arg: T): T { return arg;

}

let str = identity<string>("Hello"); let num = identity<number>(42);
```

3.3. Enums

Enums provide a convenient way to define a set of named constants, making code more descriptive and easier to understand. This is particularly useful when dealing with predefined options or status codes.

```typescript
enum Direction {


Up, Down, Left, Right,

}

let move: Direction = Direction.Up;
```

4. Migration from JavaScript to TypeScript

For JavaScript developers, transitioning to TypeScript might seem daunting. However, the migration process can be gradual, allowing teams to adopt TypeScript while still leveraging their existing JavaScript code.

4.1. Gradual Adoption

One of TypeScript's strengths is its capacity for gradual adoption. Teams can start by renaming a `.js` file to

`.ts` and adding type annotations progressively. The TypeScript compiler allows developers to specify which files should be type-checked, enabling a flexible transition.

4.2. Configuration Options

With a rich set of configuration options in the `tsconfig.json` file, teams can customize TypeScript's behavior. They can define strict type-checking options, include or exclude specific files, and manage features based on team needs or project requirements.

The power of TypeScript lies in its ability to enhance the capabilities of JavaScript, enabling developers to write more reliable, maintainable, and efficient code. As JavaScript continues to play a pivotal role in the web development ecosystem, TypeScript emerges as an invaluable ally for developers striving to tackle complexity and deliver high-quality applications.

For JavaScript developers looking to expand their toolkit, embracing TypeScript represents an investment not only in a language but in a philosophy that prioritizes clarity, precision, and collaboration. By integrating TypeScript into your development practices, you unlock a wealth of features that can significantly improve your coding experience and lead to more successful project outcomes.

typeScript for JavaScript Fundamentals

This chapter will explore TypeScript as a foundation for understanding JavaScript fundamentals, demonstrating how its features can improve the development experience and prevent common pitfalls.

Key Features of TypeScript

Static Typing: TypeScript enables developers to specify types, such as strings, numbers, and custom types. This helps catch errors at compile-time rather than runtime.

Interfaces: TypeScript allows for the definition of interfaces, which can be used to define the shape of objects. This feature is particularly useful in large applications where consistent structures are essential.

Classes and Inheritance: TypeScript supports ES6 class syntax and inheritance, providing a familiar object-oriented programming model that many developers have encountered in other languages.

Generics: Generics allow functions and classes to operate on different data types without sacrificing type safety. This promotes code reuse and flexibility.

Tooling and Integration: TypeScript's integration with popular IDEs (like Visual Studio Code) provides powerful features such as autocompletion, refactoring tools, and real-time error checking.

Transitioning from JavaScript to TypeScript

For seasoned JavaScript developers, transitioning to TypeScript may feel daunting at first. However, TypeScript is designed to be adopted gradually. The first step is to create a new TypeScript file with the extension `.ts` alongside your existing JavaScript files, allowing both languages to coexist.

A primary focus when transitioning is to understand how TypeScript enforces types. Let's compare JavaScript with TypeScript in the context of variable declarations:

JavaScript Example

```javascript
let message = "Hello, World!";

message = 42; // No error, but this can lead to bugs
```

TypeScript Example

```typescript
let message: string = "Hello, World!";

message = 42; // Error: Type 'number' is not assignable to type 'string'
```

In the TypeScript example, attempting to assign a number to `message` results in a compile-time error, helping developers identify potential issues early.

Understanding TypeScript Types

TypeScript supports a variety of data types. Here are a few of the basics:

Primitive Types: TypeScript recognizes JavaScript's primitive types, including:

`string`

`number`

`boolean`

`undefined`

`null`

`symbol` (ES6)

Array Types: You can define arrays using the following syntax:

```typescript
let numbers: number[] = [1, 2, 3];
```

Tuple Types: Tuples allow you to define an array with specific types for each index:

```typescript
let tuple: [string, number] = ["Alice", 30];
```

Union Types: A variable can hold more than one type using union types:

```typescript
let value: string | number;
```

Any Type: When unsure of a specific type, you can use the `any` type, but it's advisable to use it sparingly.

```typescript
let variable: any = "Test";
variable = 42; // No error, but loses type safety
```

```
```

Interfaces and Type Aliases

When building complex applications, defining the structure of objects becomes crucial. TypeScript provides

`interfaces` and `type aliases` for this purpose. #### Using Interfaces

```typescript
interface User { name: string; age: number;
}
const user: User = { name: "Bob",
age: 25,
};
```

Using Type Aliases

```typescript
type Point = {
x: number;

y: number;
};
const point: Point = { x: 10, y: 20 };
```

Advantages of Using TypeScript

Error Reduction: By enforcing static types, TypeScript helps reduce common errors and type-related bugs.

Enhanced Readability: Types serve as documentation, making the codebase easier for developers to understand and maintain.

Better Refactoring: With a strong type system in place, refactoring becomes less risky, as the compiler can quickly identify affected areas of the codebase.

Community and Adoption: TypeScript has gained immense popularity, with many libraries and frameworks (including Angular, React, and Vue.js) embracing it. A vibrant community ensures support and continued evolution.

TypeScript stands as an essential evolution of JavaScript, enriching developers' toolkits with features that enhance code robustness and maintainability. By understanding TypeScript, developers can build on the foundations of JavaScript while benefiting from stronger typing, better organization, and a smoother development experience.

Chapter 2: Getting Started with TypeScript for JavaScript

In this chapter, we will examine the process of initiating work with TypeScript, particularly for individuals who already possess a background in JavaScript.

Understanding TypeScript

TypeScript is an open-source programming language that is developed and supported by Microsoft. It enhances JavaScript by incorporating static typing, interfaces, and sophisticated tooling, which allows developers to create code that is more reliable and easier to maintain. As TypeScript is a superset of JavaScript, any pre-existing JavaScript code can be executed in TypeScript without any alterations.

Why Use TypeScript?

Static Typing: TypeScript introduces static types, which assist in identifying errors during the development phase rather than at runtime. This results in improved tooling and overall code quality.**Enhanced Tooling**: Features like autocompletion, code navigation, and refactoring tools are enhanced with TypeScript. IDEs like Visual Studio Code provide rich support for TypeScript, making development seamless.

Better Documentation: Type annotations in TypeScript serve as a form of documentation. When you define a function's arguments and return values explicitly, it becomes easier for other developers (or yourself in the future) to understand how to use that function.

Modern JavaScript Features: TypeScript embraces

modern JavaScript (ES6 and beyond) features and allows backward compatibility. You can use advanced features without worrying about browser support.

Improved Refactoring: The static type system makes refactoring large codebases easier and safer by providing compile-time checks.

Setting Up TypeScript ### Prerequisites

Before diving into TypeScript, you should have a basic understanding of JavaScript and Node.js installed on your machine. You can verify your installation of Node.js by running:

```bash node -v
```

Installing TypeScript

To get started with TypeScript, you can install it globally using npm (Node Package Manager). This allows you to compile TypeScript files from the command line:

```bash

npm install -g typescript


```

Once installed, you can verify the installation by checking the version:

```bash tsc -v
```

Creating Your First TypeScript File

Now that TypeScript is installed, let's create a simple TypeScript file.

Create a new directory for your project:

```bash
mkdir ts-project cd ts-project
```

Create a new TypeScript file named `app.ts`:

```typescript
// app.ts
const greet = (name: string): string => { return `Hello, ${name}!`;
};
console.log(greet('TypeScript'));
```

In this example, we define a function `greet` that takes a parameter `name` of type `string` and returns another string. The type annotations help ensure that only strings are passed to the `greet` function.

Compiling TypeScript

TypeScript code is not executed directly by the browser or Node.js; it needs to be compiled into JavaScript. To compile the `app.ts` file, you can run the TypeScript compiler (tsc) from the command line:

```bash
tsc app.ts
```

This will create a corresponding `app.js` file in the same

directory. You can now execute the compiled JavaScript file using Node.js:

```bash
node app.js
```

You should see the output: `Hello, TypeScript!`. ### TypeScript Configuration

For larger projects, it's common to include a configuration file to manage TypeScript compilation options. You can generate a `tsconfig.json` file in your project directory by running:

```bash
tsc --init
```

This file contains various settings, such as target JavaScript version, whether to include source maps, and more. Here's a simple example of what `tsconfig.json` might look like:

```json
{
"compilerOptions": { "target": "es6", "module": "commonjs", "strict": true, "sourceMap": true
},
"include": [ "src/**/*"
],
"exclude": [ "node_modules"
]
```

```
}
```
``` ` ` ```

Writing TypeScript Code

Once you have the setup ready, you can start writing TypeScript code. Here are some key concepts to explore:

Types: TypeScript supports various primitive types including `string`, `number`, `boolean`, `void`, and `any`. Additionally, you can create custom types using interfaces and type aliases.

Interfaces: Interfaces allow you to define the shape of an object. They help create contracts for classes and functions, enhancing code clarity.

```typescript
interface User {
name: string; age: number;
}
const user: User = { name: 'Alice', age: 30
};
```

Enums: TypeScript provides enums to define a set of named constants. This makes your code more readable.

```typescript
enum Color {
Red, Green,
Blue
}
const myColor: Color = Color.Green;
```
```

```
```

Generics: Generics allow you to create reusable components that can work with any data type while still maintaining type safety.

```typescript
function identity<T>(arg: T): T { return arg;

}
```

With its strong typing system and advanced features, TypeScript is an excellent choice for developing scalable and maintainable applications. In the following chapters, we will delve deeper into TypeScript's features, allowing you to leverage them effectively in your projects. Embracing TypeScript not only enhances your workflow but also prepares you for the modern development landscape. Happy coding!

Installing and Setting Up TypeScript in Your Project

TypeScript has become one of the most popular tools in the JavaScript ecosystem due to its ability to add static typing and enhanced tooling to JavaScript applications. This chapter will guide you through the step- by-step process of installing TypeScript in your project, configuring it, and ensuring that you can take full advantage of its powerful features.

Why TypeScript?

Before diving into the installation process, let's briefly

revisit why you might want to use TypeScript:

Static Typing: TypeScript's static type system helps catch errors at compile-time rather than run- time, enhancing the reliability of your code.

Improved Tooling: Modern IDEs provide better autocompletion, refactoring, and navigation capabilities with TypeScript.

Rich Ecosystem Compatibility: TypeScript integrates well with popular frameworks like React, Angular, and Vue, making it versatile for various types of projects.

Prerequisites

Before you begin, ensure you have the following requirements:

Node.js: TypeScript runs on Node.js, so you need to have it installed on your machine. You can download it from the [official Node.js website](https://nodejs.org/).

Package Manager: You can use npm (which comes with Node.js) or yarn to manage packages.

To verify your installations, open your terminal (Command Prompt, PowerShell, or terminal application) and run:

```bash node -v npm -v

```

You should see the version numbers of Node.js and npm respectively. ## Step 1: Install TypeScript Globally

To start using TypeScript, you can install it globally on your machine, which allows you to use the `tsc` command in any project. Open your terminal and run:

```bash
npm install -g typescript
```

This command installs the TypeScript compiler globally. To verify the installation, check the TypeScript version by running:

```bash tsc -v
```

You should see the version number of TypeScript displayed in the terminal. ## Step 2: Initialize Your Project

Next, you should initialize your project, which will create a `package.json` file. Navigate to your project directory (or create a new one) and run the following command:

```bash
mkdir my-typescript-project cd my-typescript-project npm init -y
```

The `-y` flag automatically answers yes to all prompts, creating a default `package.json` file. ## Step 3: Install TypeScript Locally

While global installation is useful, it's best practice to install TypeScript locally for each project. This ensures that everyone working on the project uses the same version. Run:

```bash
```

```bash
npm install --save-dev typescript
```

This command installs TypeScript as a development dependency in your project. ## Step 4: Create a TypeScript Configuration File

To set up TypeScript for your project, you need a `tsconfig.json` file. This file allows you to define various TypeScript compiler options and project structure settings. Run the following command to create a basic

`tsconfig.json` file:

```bash
npx tsc --init
```

This command generates a `tsconfig.json` file with default settings. You can customize this file according to your needs. Here's a basic example of what it might look like:

```json
{
"compilerOptions": { "target": "es6", "module": "commonjs", "strict": true, "esModuleInterop": true, "skipLibCheck": true,

"forceConsistentCasingInFileNames": true
},
"include": ["src/**/*"],


"exclude": ["node_modules", "**/*.spec.ts"]
```

}
```
```

Explanation of Key Options

`target`: Specifies the ECMAScript version to compile to (e.g., `es6`, `es5`).

`module`: Sets the module system (e.g., `commonjs`, `esnext`).

`strict`: Enable all strict type-checking options.

`esModuleInterop`: Enables emit interoperability between CommonJS and ES Modules.

`include`: Specifies the files or directories to include in the compilation.

`exclude`: Specifies the files or directories to exclude from the compilation. ## Step 5: Create Your First TypeScript File

Create a new folder in your project named `src`:

```bash mkdir src
```

Inside this folder, create a new file named `index.ts`:

```typescript
// src/index.ts

let message: string = "Hello, TypeScript!";
console.log(message);
```

Step 6: Compile Your TypeScript Code

To compile your TypeScript code into JavaScript, you can use the `tsc` command. This will read your

`tsconfig.json` file and compile the files specified in the `include` option. Run the following command in your terminal:

```bash
npx tsc
```

You should see a new folder named `dist` (if defined in the `tsconfig.json`) or the compiled JS files in the same directory as your `.ts` files.

Step 7: Run Your Compiled JavaScript Code

Now that you've compiled your TypeScript code, you can run the resulting JavaScript file using Node.js:

```bash
node dist/index.js
```

You should see `Hello, TypeScript!` printed in the terminal.

By following these outlined steps, you can start leveraging the powerful features of TypeScript to write more robust and maintainable code.

Understanding tsconfig.json and Compiler Options

When developing applications using TypeScript, one of the first files you will encounter is `tsconfig.json`. This JSON file serves as the blueprint for your TypeScript compiler settings and project configuration.

Understanding how `tsconfig.json` works and the available compiler options is crucial for effective TypeScript development. This chapter will delve into the structure of `tsconfig.json`, the purpose of various compiler options, and how to leverage them to tailor your development experience.

What is `tsconfig.json`?

The `tsconfig.json` file is a configuration file that specifies the root files and the compiler options required to compile a TypeScript project. It allows developers to define how TypeScript should process the code, control output behavior, and manage project settings, making it easier to maintain large codebases.

Structure of `tsconfig.json`

The basic structure of a `tsconfig.json` file is comprised of a few key properties:

compilerOptions: This is where you define the various settings and options for the TypeScript compiler.

include: This specifies an array of file patterns that should be included in the compilation.

exclude: This is a way to specify files or directories that should be excluded from compilation.

files: This key allows for the explicit listing of individual files to be compiled. Here is an example of a simple `tsconfig.json` file:

```json
{
```

```
"compilerOptions": {  "target":  "es6",  "module":
"commonjs", "strict": true, "esModuleInterop": true,
"outDir": "./dist"
},
"include": ["src/**/*"],

"exclude": ["node_modules", "**/*.spec.ts"]

}
```

Key Compiler Options

The `compilerOptions` property defines a wide range of
options for configuring the TypeScript compiler. Below are
some of the most commonly used options:

Target

`target`: Specifies the JavaScript version that the
TypeScript code will compile into. Common options are
`es5`, `es6`, `esnext`, etc. Setting it to `es6` will
generate ES6-compatible code.

Module

`module`: Denotes the module system to be used.
Possible values include `commonjs`, `amd`, `es6`, etc.
This is particularly important for module-based
architectures.

Strict Type-Checking Options

`strict`: When set to `true`, it enables all strict type-
checking options. This can help catch potential errors
early in the development process.

`noImplicitAny`: Disallow the usage of variables with an 'any' type unless explicitly defined. ### Output Configuration

`outDir`: Specifies the output directory for compiled JavaScript files. This helps in organizing outputs in a structured manner.

`rootDir`: This is the root directory of input files; it signifies where TypeScript starts looking for files. Setting this can help keep your project organized.

ES Module Interoperability

`esModuleInterop`: Enables emit interoperability between CommonJS and ES Modules, allowing for default imports from modules that do not have a default export.

Source Maps

`sourceMap`: When set to `true`, TypeScript generates sourceMap files that allow you to debug the original TypeScript code in the browser or other tools.

Declaration Files

`declaration`: If set to `true`, TypeScript generates declaration files (`.d.ts`) alongside the compiled files. This is useful for library development, as it helps others understand the types your library exposes.

Checking for Errors

`noFallthroughCasesInSwitch`: Enforces that all cases in a switch statement either have break statements or throw errors, helping to avoid unintended fall-through behavior.

Advanced Options

Beyond the basic options, TypeScript provides an array of advanced options that can help fine-tune your compilation process:

`skipLibCheck`: Skips type checking of declaration files (`.d.ts`), which can speed up compilation times for large projects.

`forceConsistentCasingInFileNames`: Ensures that file names are consistently cased across the entire project, mitigating potential issues in case-sensitive file systems.

`paths`: Allows for mapping of module paths to align with specific directories, streamlining the import process for external modules.

Understanding `tsconfig.json` and the various compiler options available empowers developers to configure their TypeScript projects effectively. By leveraging the options detailed in this chapter, you can improve the maintainability, performance, and quality of your TypeScript code. As you gain more experience, you can explore and experiment with different settings to find the best configurations that suit your specific project needs.

Chapter 3: TypeScript's Powerful Type System

In this chapter, we will explore the features and advantages of TypeScript's type system, how it enhances code quality, and why it has become an essential tool for many developers.

3.1 Understanding TypeScript's Type System

At its core, TypeScript builds upon JavaScript by introducing static typing. This means that developers can define types for their variables, function parameters, return values, and more before the code is even executed. This proactive approach allows for better documentation, code predictability, and reduced runtime errors.

3.1.1 Basic Types

TypeScript provides several built-in types that developers can leverage to describe their data. These include:

Number: Represents both integer and floating-point numbers.

String: Represents a sequence of characters.

Boolean: Represents a true/false value.

Array: Represents a collection of elements of a specific type, e.g., `number[]`, `string[]`.

Tuple: Represents an array with fixed number of elements, where each element can be of different types.

Enum: Represents a set of named constants, allowing for a more meaningful representation of numeric values.

Any: A fallback type that allows a variable to hold

values of any type.

This variety enables developers to create strongly typed variables which can significantly reduce bugs during development.

3.1.2 Type Inference

One of the most powerful aspects of TypeScript is its type inference feature. Even when types are not explicitly defined, TypeScript can often infer the types based on the assigned values. For example:

```typescript
let num = 10; // Type inferred as number

let name = "Alice"; // Type inferred as string
```

This reduces the need for excessive type annotations while still leveraging the advantages of a type system. It allows developers to write cleaner, more concise code while retaining the benefits of type-checking.

3.2 Advanced Type Features

TypeScript's powerful type system goes beyond basic types, providing advanced features that enable developers to create more flexible and robust applications.

3.2.1 Interfaces

Interfaces are a cornerstone of TypeScript's type system, allowing developers to define contracts for objects:

```typescript interface User {
```

```typescript
id: number; name: string; email: string;
}
const user: User = { id: 1,
name: "Alice",
email: "alice@example.com"
};
```

Interfaces not only enhance code readability and maintainability, but they also promote a strong adherence to object-oriented programming paradigms.

3.2.2 Union and Intersection Types

TypeScript allows for union types, which enable variables to hold multiple types, enhancing flexibility:

```typescript
let value: string | number; value = "Hello"; // valid value = 42; // valid
```

On the other hand, intersection types allow for combining multiple types into one, providing more comprehensive type definitions:

```typescript
interface Person {
name: string;
}
interface Employee { employeeId: number;
}
```

```typescript
type EmployeePerson = Person & Employee; const emp:
EmployeePerson = {
name: "Bob", employeeId: 12345
};
```

These features empower developers to create rich models that mirror real-world scenarios. ### 3.2.3 Generics

Generics are a way to create reusable components that can work with any data type. They allow developers to define functions, classes, and interfaces that can operate on various data types while retaining full type safety:

```typescript
function identity<T>(arg: T): T { return arg;
}
let result = identity<string>("Hello");
```

Generics provide flexibility without losing the benefits of static typing, making the codebase more adaptable and easier to maintain.

3.3 TypeScript and Error Reduction

One of the most significant advantages of TypeScript's type system is its potential to reduce errors during development. By catching type-related issues at compile-time rather than runtime, developers can identify bugs early in the development process, leading to a smoother and more efficient development cycle.

3.3.1 Type Safety in Functions

In TypeScript, developers can enforce type safety in function signatures, ensuring that functions receive the expected types of parameters and return values:

```typescript
function add(x: number, y: number): number { return x +
y;
}
let result = add(5, 10); // Valid
let invalidResult = add("5", 10); // Error: Argument of type 'string' is not assignable to parameter of type 'number'.
```

This early detection of type mismatches not only saves time but also leads to more reliable code as applications grow in complexity.

By adopting TypeScript, developers can not only improve code quality but also foster better collaboration within teams, as the explicit type definitions serve as excellent documentation and aid in understanding codebases.

Primitive and Complex Types (string, number, boolean, object, any, never, unknown)

Understanding the difference between primitive and complex types is essential for effectively leveraging TypeScript in software development. In this chapter, we'll explore the primitive types—string, number, boolean—and the complex types—object, any, never, and unknown.

1. Primitive Types

Primitive types are the basic building blocks of data in TypeScript. They represent single values and have immutable characteristics. Let's look at the primitive types provided by TypeScript:

1.1 String

The `string` type is used to represent textual data. Strings can be defined using single quotes, double quotes, or backticks (for template literals).

```typescript
let greeting: string = "Hello, TypeScript!"; let name: string = 'John Doe';

let ageStatement: string = `My name is ${name} and I am 30 years old.`;
```

1.2 Number

TypeScript utilizes the JavaScript `number` type for all numeric values, including integers and floating-point numbers. There is no distinction between them, as TypeScript uses double-precision 64-bit binary format.

```typescript
let age: number = 30;

let price: number = 29.99;

let population: number = 7_900_000_000; // Using underscores for readability
```

1.3 Boolean

The `boolean` type is used to represent a logical entity that can only be true or false. This type is crucial for controlling the flow of logic in applications, such as in conditional statements.

```typescript
let isAvailable: boolean = true; let isActive: boolean = false;
```

2. Complex Types

Complex types represent more intricate structures and can encompass multiple values or relationships between values. Let's explore the complex types available in TypeScript:

2.1 Object

The `object` type is used to represent a non-primitive type that can take on various forms, such as arrays, functions, and more complex data structures. It allows for a flexible way to work with various types of objects.

```typescript
let person: object = { name: "Alice", age: 28, isEmployed: true

};

// Accessing properties

console.log(person.name); // TypeScript will report an error if you try to access properties that are not explicitly typed.
```

```
```

2.2 Any

The `any` type is a wildcard that allows you to opt-out of type checking. It can hold any value of any type, making it highly flexible but potentially dangerous. Overusing `any` can lead to runtime errors that would otherwise be caught at compile time.

```typescript
let randomValue: any = 42;

randomValue = "A string now"; // No error randomValue = false; // Still no error
```

2.3 Never

The `never` type represents values that will never occur. This could happen in scenarios such as throwing an error or an infinite loop. The `never` type provides a way to indicate the absence of a return value, particularly for functions that do not complete normally.

```typescript
function throwError(message: string): never { throw new Error(message);

}
```

2.4 Unknown

The `unknown` type is a safer alternative to `any`. It represents any value but requires type checking before performing operations on it. This makes the code more type-safe compared to using `any`.

```typescript
let uncertainValue: unknown = 42;

if (typeof uncertainValue === "string") {
console.log(uncertainValue.toUpperCase()); // Safe to call toUpperCase

} else {

console.log("Not a string!");

}
```

In this chapter, we explored the fundamental building blocks of TypeScript's type system, distinguishing between primitive types like `string`, `number`, and `boolean`, and complex types such as `object`, `any`,

`never`, and `unknown`.

Understanding these types will not only enhance code quality but also serve as a robust foundation for developing more complex applications. Familiarizing yourself with how and when to use these types is crucial for building maintainable and error-resistant applications in TypeScript. In the upcoming chapters, we will delve into type inference, type aliases, and advanced type manipulations to further enhance your TypeScript expertise.

Type Inference vs Explicit Typing

One of the fascinating and powerful features of TypeScript

is its approach to typing. This chapter explores two primary methods of handling data types in TypeScript: type inference and explicit typing.

What is Type Inference?

Type inference is a mechanism by which TypeScript automatically deduces the type of a variable based on its initial value. When you assign a value to a variable, TypeScript analyzes the value and determines its type. This allows developers to write code without having to specify types explicitly, thereby reducing verbosity and keeping the code clean and concise.

How Type Inference Works

TypeScript employs a set of rules to infer types based on the context. Here are some scenarios where type inference is applied:

Basic Variable Assignment: TypeScript infers the type from the value assigned.

```typescript
let str = "Hello, TypeScript"; // Type inferred as string let
num = 42;    // Type inferred as number
```

Function Return Types: When a function returns a value, TypeScript can infer the return type.

```typescript
function add(a: number, b: number) {

return a + b; // Return type inferred as number

}
```

```

```

Array and Object Literals: When declaring arrays or objects, TypeScript infers types based on their structure.

```typescript
let arr = [1, 2, 3];     // Type inferred as number[]

let obj = { name: "Alice", age: 30 }; // Type inferred as {
name: string; age: number }
```

Advantages of Type Inference

Reduced Boilerplate: Developers can write less code since they do not need to repeatedly specify types.

Maintainability: Type inference makes the code easier to read and manage, especially in large codebases.

Reduced Errors: By inferring types, TypeScript can still provide type-checking benefits without requiring explicit definitions.

What is Explicit Typing?

Explicit typing, as the name suggests, involves defining the type of a variable or a function signature explicitly. This is particularly useful when the intended type is not clear from the context, or if a developer wants to enforce a specific type for better control.

How Explicit Typing Works

Explicit typing is done using a colon followed by the type after the variable name or in the function signature. Here are some examples:

Declaring Variables: We can explicitly define types for

variables.

```typescript
let name: string = "John Doe"; // Explicitly specifying
type as string let age: number = 25;      //      Explicitly
specifying type as number
```

Function Signatures: Function parameters and return types can be explicitly defined.

```typescript
function multiply(a: number, b: number): number {

return a * b; // Return type explicitly declared as number

}
```

Object Types: You can specify complex object types explicitly, enhancing clarity and intention.

```typescript interface User {

name: string; age: number;

}

let user: User = { name: "Alice", age: 30 }; // Explicitly
defining type
```

Advantages of Explicit Typing

Clarity and Intent: It makes your code self-documenting. Future readers (including yourself) will have a clearer understanding of what types are expected.

Precise Control: It provides more control over the types, especially in complex applications where inference might lead to unexpected types or errors.

Enhanced IDE Support: Explicit types can improve the feedback from IDEs, providing better autocompletion and type-checking capabilities.

Type Inference vs Explicit Typing

While both type inference and explicit typing have their advantages, understanding when to use each is crucial for effective TypeScript development.

When to Prefer Type Inference

When the type is clear from the context and does not need to be enforced.

To keep the code concise and enhance readability.

In prototypes or smaller scripts where verbosity can hinder productivity.

When to Prefer Explicit Typing

When the intent of the type needs to be unmistakably clear.

In public APIs or libraries, where consumers may not have the same context as the library developer.

In complex structures or when dealing with unknowns (e.g., API responses), where clarity is essential.

Understanding the interplay between type inference and explicit typing in TypeScript is vital for maximizing the benefits of the language's type system. Both methods serve their purposes, with type inference offering convenience and explicit typing providing clarity and precision. Striking the right balance between the two can lead to more robust, maintainable, and readable code.

Chapter 4: Mastering Functions in TypeScript

In TypeScript, functions become even more powerful and adaptable thanks to its strong typing system and features that help in developing more maintainable and scalable applications. This chapter aims to deepen your understanding of functions in TypeScript — covering function declarations, expressions, parameters, return types, and more advanced concepts such as higher-order functions, decorators, and async functions.

4.1 Function Declarations and Expressions

Functions in TypeScript can be defined in several ways: function declarations, function expressions, and arrow functions.

4.1.1 Function Declarations

A function declaration consists of the `function` keyword followed by the function name, a list of parameters in parentheses, and a block of code.

```typescript
function greet(name: string): string { return `Hello,
${name}!`;
}
```

In this example, we defined a function called `greet` that takes a parameter `name` of type `string` and returns a `string`.

4.1.2 Function Expressions

Function expressions allow us to create functions within variable assignments. Here's how you define a function expression:

```typescript
const greet = function(name: string): string { return `Hello, ${name}!`;
};
```

4.1.3 Arrow Functions

An alternative and more concise way to write function expressions is using arrow functions.

```typescript
const greet = (name: string): string => `Hello, ${name}!`;
```

Arrow functions have the added benefit of not binding their own `this`, which can be advantageous in certain contexts.

4.2 Parameters and Default Values

TypeScript allows us to define the types of parameters explicitly, enhancing code readability and preventing bugs. Moreover, TypeScript supports default parameter values.

```typescript
function greet(name: string = 'Visitor'): string { return `Hello, ${name}!`;
}
```

```
```

If no argument is provided for `name`, it defaults to the string `"Visitor"`. ### 4.2.1 Rest Parameters

Sometimes, functions need to accept an unspecified number of arguments. TypeScript supports this through rest parameters.

```typescript
function sum(...numbers: number[]): number {

return numbers.reduce((total, num) => total + num, 0);

}
```

In this example, `sum` can take any number of numeric arguments and calculates their total. ## 4.3 Return Types

In TypeScript, we can explicitly define the return type of functions, improving code clarity.

```typescript
function square(num: number): number { return num *
num;

}
```

If a function does not return a value, its return type should be specified as `void`.

```typescript
function log(message: string): void { console.log(message);

}
```

```
```

4.4 Higher-Order Functions

Higher-order functions are functions that either accept other functions as arguments or return functions. They are a key aspect of functional programming and can lead to more concise and expressive code.

Example of a Higher-Order Function

```typescript
function applyOperation(a: number, b: number, operation: (x: number, y: number) => number): number {
return operation(a, b);

}

const result = applyOperation(5, 10, (x, y) => x + y); // result equals 15
```

In this example, `applyOperation` takes two number arguments and a function that performs an operation on those numbers.

4.5 Function Overloading

TypeScript supports function overloading, allowing you to define multiple signatures for the same function name. This is particularly useful when dealing with varying input types.

Example of Function Overloading

```typescript
function combine(input: string, input2: string): string;
function combine(input: number, input2: number):
```

```
number; function combine(input: any, input2: any): any {
return input + input2;
}
```
```

Here, the `combine` function can accept two strings and return a string or accept two numbers and return a number.

## 4.6 Async Functions

With the rise of asynchronous programming, TypeScript provides native support for `async` functions, which return a promise. This is particularly useful for tasks that require time-consuming operations like network requests.

### Example of an Async Function

```typescript
async function fetchUser(id: number): Promise<User> {
const response = await fetch(`https://api.example.com/users/${id}`); return await response.json();
}
```

In this example, `fetchUser` fetches user data asynchronously, returning a promise that resolves to a `User` object.

4.7 Decorators and Functions

TypeScript supports decorators, which are special annotations that can modify classes and their members,
```

including methods. Utilizing decorators effectively can enhance the functionality of your functions.

Example of a Simple Method Decorator

```typescript
function log(target: any, key: string, descriptor: PropertyDescriptor) { const originalMethod = descriptor.value;

descriptor.value = function (...args: any[]) {

console.log(`Calling ${key} with arguments: ${JSON.stringify(args)}`);


return originalMethod.apply(this, args);

};

}

class Example { @log

add(x: number, y: number): number { return x + y;

}

}
```

In this case, the `log` decorator modifies the `add` method to log its arguments before executing.

Understanding functions in TypeScript is essential for writing efficient, maintainable, and type-safe code. As you have learned, TypeScript enhances standard JavaScript functions with strong typing, higher-order functionalities, and more.

Strongly Typed Function Parameters and Return Types

With its rise, so too has the demand for more structure and safety in programming. This is where TypeScript steps in. TypeScript, developed by Microsoft, builds on JavaScript by adding static typing, enabling developers to catch errors at compile time rather than runtime. One of the most powerful features of TypeScript lies in its capability to declare strongly typed function parameters and return types. This chapter delves into these features, exploring their significance, syntax, and practical application, ultimately illustrating how they can unleash the full potential of JavaScript development.

The Importance of Strong Typing

Strong typing in programming refers to the enforcement of strict rules regarding data types, which ensures that variables and functions operate predictably. The key benefits of using strongly typed function parameters and return types include:

Error Reduction: By specifying types, developers can avoid common bugs that arise from unexpected data types.

Enhanced Readability: Strong typing enhances code clarity, as it provides documentation on what types of parameters are expected and what the function will return.

Improved Tooling Support: Many IDEs and text

editors can provide better autocompletion and type-checking features when the data types are explicitly defined.

Ease of Refactoring: Strong types make it easier to refactor code, as the compiler can alert the developer to mismatched types before the code is run.

Basic Syntax

Function Parameters

In TypeScript, you can specify the type of each parameter in a function by appending a colon followed by the type after the parameter name. The syntax looks like this:

```typescript
function greet(name: string): void { console.log(`Hello,
${name}!`);

}
```

In this example, `name` is defined as a parameter of type `string`. If a caller attempts to pass a different data type, TypeScript will throw a compile-time error.

Return Types

While it is optional to specify a return type in TypeScript (the compiler can infer it), doing so can improve the clarity of your code. The return type follows the parameter definitions and is preceded by a colon:

```typescript
function add(a: number, b: number): number { return a +
```

```
b;
}
```
` ` `

Here, the `add` function expects two parameters (`a` and `b`) of type `number` and guarantees the return type will also be a `number`.

Optional and Default Parameters

TypeScript also supports optional parameters and default parameters, which enhance function flexibility:

Optional Parameters - These can be defined using a question mark `?`:

` ` `typescript

```
function greet(name: string, age?: number): void { if (age)
{
console.log(`Hello, ${name}! You are ${age} years old.`);
} else {
console.log(`Hello, ${name}!`);
}
}
```
` ` `

Default Parameters - These allow a parameter to have a default value if no argument is provided:

` ` `typescript

```
function greet(name: string, greeting: string = "Hello"):
void { console.log(`${greeting}, ${name}!`);
```

```
}
```

Practical Examples

Example 1: User Registration

Let's consider a function that registers users. We can define a function that accepts an object parameter representing user details and explicitly state the expected types:

```typescript
interface User {
```

username: string; email: string; password: string;

```
}
```

function registerUser(user: User): string {

// Simulated registration logic

return `User ${user.username} registered with email ${user.email}.`;

```
}
```

// Example usage

const newUser: User = {

username: "john_doe", email: "john@example.com", password: "securePassword"

```
};
```

console.log(registerUser(newUser));
```

```

The `User` interface defines the structure of the user

object, and the `registerUser` function takes this object as a parameter, ensuring type safety.

Example 2: Functional Programming with Callbacks

TypeScript excels in functional programming scenarios, especially when dealing with callbacks. Here's an example of a function that processes an array of numbers with a callback function:

```typescript
function processNumbers(numbers: number[], callback: (num: number) => number): number[] { return numbers.map(callback);

}

const doubled = processNumbers([1, 2, 3, 4], (num: number) => num * 2);

console.log(doubled); // [2, 4, 6, 8]
```

In this example, the `callback` parameter is a function that receives a number and returns a number, ensuring that only valid callback functions can be passed.

By embracing type annotations, developers can greatly reduce the chances of runtime errors, improve documentation for each function, and leverage tooling that enhances the development experience.

Function Overloading and Advanced Typing in Functions

This chapter delves into these concepts, illustrating how developers can leverage TypeScript's typing system to create cleaner, more predictable code.

1. Understanding Function Overloading

Function overloading allows you to create multiple signatures for a single function, providing varied ways to invoke the function based on the types and numbers of its parameters. Unlike Java, TypeScript does not enforce overloads at runtime; it uses static typing to offer compile-time checks instead.

1.1 Basic Syntax of Function Overloading

In TypeScript, you can define multiple call signatures for a function followed by a single implementation.

```typescript
function greet(person: string): string;

function greet(person: string, age: number): string;
function greet(person: string, age?: number): string {

if (age !== undefined) {

return `Hello, ${person}. You are ${age} years old.`;

}

return `Hello, ${person}!`;

}

// Usage

console.log(greet("Alice"));        //      Hello,      Alice!
console.log(greet("Bob", 30)); // Hello, Bob. You are 30 years old.
```

```

```

In this example, we have overloaded the `greet` function to handle both a single parameter (a string) and two parameters (a string and a number). The overloads provide flexibility in how we can use `greet`.

1.2 Benefits of Function Overloading

Readability: Overloading allows you to express different behaviors of a function without cluttering your code with multiple function names.

Type Safety: TypeScript enforces type checks at compile time, ensuring that the correct parameters are passed, thus reducing potential runtime errors.

Intuition: It makes APIs easier to understand because related functionalities are grouped under the same function name.

2. Advanced Typing in Functions

TypeScript offers a rich type system that can enhance your function definitions in multiple ways. ### 2.1 Union Types

Union types allow a function to accept parameters of multiple types. For instance, you can define a function that accepts either a string or a number:

```typescript
function formatValue(value: string | number): string {

return typeof value === "number" ? value.toFixed(2) : value.toUpperCase();

}
```

```
// Usage
console.log(formatValue("hello"));      //      HELLO
console.log(formatValue(123.456)); // 123.46
```

This function can be used seamlessly with either string or number inputs, with TypeScript ensuring type correctness.

2.2 Function Types

You can define a function type that has specific parameter types and a return type. This is useful when you want to pass functions as arguments or store them in variables.

```typescript
type Callback = (data: string) => void;

function processData(data: string, callback: Callback): void {

// Simulated processing

const        processedData       =        data.toUpperCase();
callback(processedData);

}

// Usage

processData("hello", (result) => { console.log(result); // HELLO

});
```

Here, we've defined a `Callback` type, ensuring that any function passed as `callback` will adhere to the expected signature.

2.3 Generics

Generics enable you to create reusable functions that work with various data types. They are a powerful way to maintain type safety while providing flexibility.

```typescript
function identity<T>(arg: T): T { return arg;
}
// Usage
const numberId = identity<number>(42); // 42 const stringId = identity<string>("Hello"); // Hello
```

In this example, the `identity` function returns an input of any type, allowing for consistent type inference depending on the parameter passed.

2.4 Rest Parameters and Tuples

TypeScript supports rest parameters, allowing a function to accept a variable number of arguments and defining them as tuples for stronger typing.

```typescript
function logMessages(...messages: [string, number, ...boolean[]]): void { console.log("String:", messages[0]);

console.log("Number:", messages[1]);
console.log("Booleans:", messages.slice(2));
}
// Usage
```

```
logMessages("Test", 42, true, false, true);
// String: Test
// Number: 42
// Booleans: [ true, false, true ]
```
```
` ` `
```

Here, we see how we can combine tuples with rest parameters to create flexible function definitions. ## 3. Best Practices

3.1 Keep Overloads Meaningful

While overloads can improve readability, ensure that they convey meaningful variations of behavior. Avoid creating too many overloads as this can lead to confusion.

3.2 Leverage Descriptive Names

When creating overloaded functions, consider using descriptive names that inform the consumer what each overload does, where appropriate.

3.3 Documentation and Type Annotation

Always provide comments or documentation for functions with multiple overloads or complex typings. This helps other developers (and your future self) understand the intended usage quickly.

By utilizing these features, developers can create flexible APIs while enjoying the benefits of type safety. As you continue your journey with TypeScript, mastering these concepts will empower you to write cleaner, more maintainable code, helping bridge the gap between simple JavaScript and robust application development.

Chapter 5: Working with Objects and Interfaces

This chapter delves into the nature of objects in TypeScript, outlines the significance of interfaces, and elucidates how these concepts can optimize JavaScript development.

5.1 Understanding Objects in TypeScript

In JavaScript, an object is a collection of key-value pairs, where keys are strings (or Symbols) and values can be any data type, including other objects or functions. TypeScript enhances object manipulation by introducing static types, which allows developers to define the structure of objects in a more predictable manner.

Creating Objects

You can create objects in TypeScript using object literals, constructors, or classes. Here's a simple example using object literals:

```typescript
const person = {
name: "John Doe", age: 30, isEmployed: true
};
```

Typed Objects

For greater control, you can explicitly type objects using TypeScript's type annotations:

```typescript
type Person = {
name: string; age: number;
```

```
isEmployed: boolean;
};
const employee: Person = { name: "Jane Smith",
age: 28, isEmployed: true
};
```

By defining the structure of the `Person` type, TypeScript will enforce type checks, helping to catch errors at compile-time.

5.2 Interfaces in TypeScript

Interfaces are one of TypeScript's powerful features that allow you to define custom types with specific structures. They establish a contract for the objects that implement them, thereby enhancing the code's readability and maintainability.

Defining an Interface

You can create an interface using the `interface` keyword. Here's how you can define an interface for a person:

```typescript
interface IPerson {
name: string; age: number; greet(): string;
}
```

In this example, `IPerson` mandates that any object implementing the interface must include two properties (`name` and `age`) and a method (`greet`).

Implementing an Interface

You can then create a class or an object that implements this interface:

```typescript
class Employee implements IPerson {

constructor(public name: string, public age: number) {}

greet(): string {

return `Hello, my name is ${this.name}.`;

}

}

const employee1 = new Employee("Alice", 35);
console.log(employee1.greet()); // Output: Hello, my name is Alice.

```

In this class example, the `Employee` class implements the `IPerson` interface. TypeScript ensures that

`Employee` adheres to the structure defined by `IPerson`, fulfilling its requirements for properties and methods.

5.3 Extending Interfaces

Interfaces in TypeScript can be extended, enabling you to build more complex types from existing ones. This feature promotes reusability and helps maintain a clean codebase.

Example of Interface Extension

Suppose you have a base interface and want to create a new interface that includes additional properties:

```typescript
```

```typescript
interface IEmployee extends IPerson { department: string;
}
const manager: IEmployee = { name: "Bob Johnson",
age: 40,
department: "HR", greet(): string {
return `Hello, my name is ${this.name} and I work in ${this.department}.`;
}
};
```

The `IEmployee` interface extends `IPerson`, adding the `department` property. This ensures that any object of type `IEmployee` contains all properties of `IPerson` plus its own.

5.4 Using Generic Interfaces

Generics in TypeScript allow you to create reusable components that can work with a variety of data types. This feature is particularly useful when working with interfaces.

Defining a Generic Interface

You can define a generic interface by adding type parameters, enabling you to create more flexible types:

```typescript
interface Response<T> { status: number;
data: T;
}
```

```
const userResponse: Response<{ name: string; age:
number }> = { status: 200,

data: { name: "Charlie", age: 25 }

};
```
` ` `

In this example, the `Response<T>` interface can work
with any data type by passing it as a type argument. This is
especially helpful in scenarios such as handling API
responses.

Working with objects and interfaces in TypeScript
provides developers with powerful tools to manage data
structures effectively. By enforcing types and allowing
interfaces to define contracts for objects, TypeScript
enhances the development process, making code more
predictable and less error-prone.

Defining and Extending Interfaces for Cleaner Code

TypeScript, a superset of JavaScript, brings strong typing
and interfaces to the table, enabling developers to define
and manage the structure of their code more effectively.
In this chapter, we will delve into how defining and
extending interfaces in TypeScript can lead to cleaner
code, particularly when working with JavaScript
codebases.

Understanding Interfaces in TypeScript

An interface in TypeScript is a powerful way to define the

shape of an object. It specifies what properties, methods, and structures an object must adhere to, enabling better type checking, code documentation, and the facilitation of refactoring. Here's a simple example of an interface:

```typescript
interface User {
id: number; name: string; email: string;
}
```

In this example, the `User` interface defines three properties: `id`, `name`, and `email`. Any object that claims to have the type `User` must include these properties with the specified types.

Why Use Interfaces?

Type Safety: Interfaces provide type safety, ensuring that objects adhere to the defined shape, which reduces runtime errors.

Autocompletion and Documentation: Tools like editors and IDEs can utilize interfaces to provide autocompletion, making development faster and more efficient.

Code Clarity: Interfaces serve as a form of documentation, clearly defining what an object should look like without requiring complex comments.

Extending Interfaces

One of the standout features of TypeScript's interfaces is the ability to extend them. This allows for more flexibility and reuse, essential in large applications. Consider the following example:

```typescript
interface Admin extends User { role: string;
}
const adminUser: Admin = { id: 1,
name: 'Alice',
email: 'alice@example.com', role: 'administrator'
};

```

In this code snippet, the `Admin` interface extends the `User` interface, adding a new property `role`. By extending interfaces, we can create richer object types while maintaining a clean and organized structure.

Use Cases for Extending Interfaces

Hierarchical Structures: In applications where entities share common properties but have additional unique attributes, extending interfaces allows developers to create a hierarchy of interfaces that reflect this relationship.

Third-Party Libraries: When integrating with third-party libraries, developers can create extended interfaces to fit their specific use cases without altering the original interfaces.

Versioning: As software evolves, extending interfaces enables versioning of data structures without breaking existing code.

Achieving Clean Code Through Interfaces

The integration of interfaces into your TypeScript codebase can significantly enhance the cleanliness and maintainability of your JavaScript applications. Here are some strategies to consider:

1. Defining Clear Interfaces

Ensure every object has a well-defined interface. This practice allows developers to understand the expectations and behaviors of objects at a glance. It can be especially beneficial in large teams or open- source projects where many different contributors interact with the code.

2. Using Optional Properties

TypeScript allows the definition of optional properties using the `?` modifier. This can lead to cleaner interfaces by encapsulating complexity in a flexible manner:

```typescript
interface Product {

id: number; name: string; price: number;

description?: string; // optional property

}
```

In this case, the `description` property is optional, allowing for products that may not require a description, thus making the interface cleaner.

3. Leveraging Indexable Types

If you're dealing with collections of objects where the keys are dynamic, TypeScript's indexable types can be utilized. This approach helps to define a cleaner structure, especially in cases where values are uniform:

```typescript
interface StringMap{ [key: string]: string;
}
```

Here, `StringMap` defines that for every key of type `string`, the corresponding value will also be of type `string`.

Defining and extending interfaces in TypeScript plays a vital role in promoting cleaner and more maintainable code in JavaScript applications. Through the use of clear, structured interfaces, developers can achieve better type safety, utilize documentation capabilities, and create scalable architectures.

Using Type Aliases and Intersection Types for Flexibility

This chapter delves into how developers can leverage these features in TypeScript to enhance the way they write JavaScript, ensuring more robust and maintainable applications.

Understanding Type Aliases

First, let's explore Type Aliases. A Type Alias is a way to give a type a new name, which can be particularly useful for making complex types more readable. It acts somewhat like a synonym, allowing you to define a specific type structure and reuse it throughout your codebase.

Declaring Type Aliases

Type Aliases are declared using the `type` keyword followed by the name of the alias and the type definition. Here's a simple example:

```typescript
type User = {
id: number; name: string; email: string;
};
const user: User = { id: 1,
name: 'John Doe',
email: 'john.doe@example.com'
};
```

In this example, we define a `User` type that includes three properties: `id`, `name`, and `email`. This alias not only improves the readability of the code but also makes it easier to reuse the `User` type across different components or functions.

Benefits of Type Aliases

Readability: Type aliases can make your code more readable, especially when dealing with complex objects or function signatures.

Reusability: Instead of repeating type definitions, you can create reusable aliases that can be referenced wherever needed, ensuring consistency.

Abstraction: They allow abstracting complex types into simpler names, helping developers understand the purpose and structure of the data being handled.

Exploring Intersection Types

Intersection Types allow you to combine multiple types into one. This means that you can create a type that has all the properties of the combined types. This feature offers significant flexibility and can help in scenarios where you want to ensure that objects conform to multiple contracts.

Declaring Intersection Types

Intersection Types are created using the ampersand (`&`) operator. Here is a practical example:

```typescript
type Vehicle = {
wheels: number; engine: string;
};
type Car = Vehicle & { doors: number; trunk: boolean;
};
const myCar: Car = { wheels: 4,
engine: 'V8', doors: 4, trunk: true
};
```

In this example, we have a `Vehicle` type and a `Car` type that extends `Vehicle` by including additional properties. The `Car` type includes `wheels` and `engine` from `Vehicle` as well as its own specific properties.

Use Cases for Intersection Types

Combining Related Types: Intersection Types allow you to combine types that represent related business concepts. For example, you might want to combine a `User` type with a `Permissions` type to create a `Admin` type that captures both user-specific and permission-specific attributes.

Advanced Object Structures: They enable developers to create more complex data structures without losing the clarity and maintainability of their code.

Type Check: They allow for stringent type checking. When you require that a type must conform to multiple interfaces, intersection types ensure that all necessary properties are fulfilled.

Practical Example: Using Alias and Intersection Types Together

Now, let's combine both Type Aliases and Intersection Types to demonstrate how to create a flexible structure that can accommodate various functionalities.

```typescript
type Address = {
```

street: string; city: string; zipCode: string;

```
};
```

type ContactInfo = { email: string; phone: string;

```
};
```

type UserProfile = User & Address & ContactInfo; const userProfile: UserProfile = {

id: 1,

```
  name: 'Jane Smith',
  email: 'jane.smith@example.com', phone: '123-456-7890',
  street: '123 Main St', city: 'Anytown', zipCode: '12345'
};
```
```

In this example, we created a `UserProfile` type that combines properties from the `User`, `Address`, and

`ContactInfo` types. This not only organizes the code better but also enforces a structure that makes it easier to understand and manage user-related data.

As TypeScript continues to gain traction in the development community, understanding and employing Type Aliases and Intersection Types becomes increasingly critical. These features empower developers to create flexible, maintainable, and readable code, enhancing collaboration and reducing bugs. Developers transitioning from JavaScript to TypeScript will find that harnessing the power of these types allows them to write more robust applications, ensuring greater compatibility and performance.
```

Chapter 6: Advanced TypeScript Features for Scalable Code

One such advancement is TypeScript, a statically typed superset of JavaScript. While many developers enjoy the benefits of TypeScript's type system, there are numerous advanced features that can lead to more scalable and maintainable code. In this chapter, we will delve into these features, examining how they can be leveraged to improve the architecture of your JavaScript applications.

6.1 Embracing Type Inference

TypeScript offers an advanced type inference system that can significantly reduce the need for explicit type annotations. When you declare variables, function parameters, or return types, TypeScript automatically infers their types based on the assigned values.

Example:

```typescript
let message = "Hello, TypeScript"; // TypeScript infers the type as string message = 42; // Error: Type 'number' is not assignable to type 'string'
```

Leveraging type inference can make your code cleaner and more expressive, allowing you to focus on the logic rather than getting bogged down in type definitions.

6.2 Union and Intersection Types

Union and intersection types are powerful features in TypeScript that allow for greater flexibility in your codebase.

Union Types

A union type allows a variable to hold multiple types. This is particularly useful for functions that can accept various data types as arguments.

```typescript
function logMessage(message: string | number) {
console.log(message);
}
```

Intersection Types

Intersection types enable you to combine multiple types into one. This is especially handy when creating objects that must adhere to multiple interfaces.

```typescript
interface User {
id: number; name: string;
}

interface Admin { role: string;
}

type AdminUser = User & Admin; const admin: AdminUser = {
id: 1,
name: "Alice",
role: "Administrator"
};
```

Using union and intersection types enhances the fluidity of your code and ensures type safety without sacrificing flexibility.

6.3 Generics for Reusability

Generics allow you to create reusable components that can work with a variety of types instead of a single one. This feature promotes code scalability by enabling the creation of more abstract and flexible code constructs.

Example of a Generic Function

```typescript
function identity<T>(arg: T): T { return arg;

}

let result = identity<string>("Hello, Generics!"); // result is of type string

```

By utilizing generics, you can create functions, classes, or interfaces that can work on any data type, reducing code duplication and increasing maintainability.

6.4 Decorators for Code Enhancement

Decorators are a special kind of declaration that can modify classes and their members. They are a powerful way to attach additional behavior to your codebase without direct modification.

Example of a Decorator

```typescript
function Log(target: any, propertyName: string, descriptor: PropertyDescriptor) { const originalMethod =
```

```typescript
descriptor.value;
descriptor.value = function(...args: any[]) {
console.log(`Method ${propertyName} called with args:
${args}`); return originalMethod.apply(this, args);
};
}
class Example { @Log
sum(a: number, b: number) {
return a + b;
}
}
const example = new Example();
example.sum(5, 10); // Logs: Method sum called with
args: 5,10
```

Using decorators can improve the modularity of your code, making it easier to enhance and manage behaviors separately from the core logic.

6.5 Type Aliases and Utility Types

Type aliases allow you to create a new name for a type, enhancing readability and maintainability. ### Example of Type Alias

```typescript
typescript type Point = {
x: number; y: number;
};
```

```
const point: Point = { x: 10, y: 20 };
```

Additionally, TypeScript offers several built-in utility types that can simplify common type transformations, such as `Partial`, `Readonly`, `Record`, and more. These utility types can significantly reduce boilerplate and enhance type manipulation.

Example of Utility Types

```typescript
interface User {

id: number; name: string; email?: string;

}

type PartialUser = Partial<User>; // All properties are optional

type ReadonlyUser = Readonly<User>; // All properties are readonly
```

6.6 Advanced Conditional Types

Conditional types allow you to express non-uniform type semantics. This feature is ideal for cases where the type depends on a condition.

Example of a Conditional Type

```typescript
type IsString<T> = T extends string ? 'Yes' : 'No';

type A = IsString<string>; // Result is 'Yes' type B = IsString<number>; // Result is 'No'
```

```
```

Conditional types open up new possibilities for type manipulation, enabling you to express complex type dependencies in a clean manner.

By utilizing type inference, union and intersection types, generics, decorators, utility types, and conditional types, developers can build robust applications capable of growing over time without losing clarity or performance.

Working with Union and Literal Types for Safer Code

In this chapter, we will explore Union and Literal Types in TypeScript, how they can be used to create safer, more predictable code, and how they can enhance the developer's experience when working with JavaScript.

Understanding Union Types

Union types allow you to define a variable that can hold values of multiple types. This can be particularly useful when you're dealing with functions that can accept different types of arguments or when certain variables can represent different forms of data.

Defining Union Types

In TypeScript, you can define a union type by using the pipe (`|`) symbol. For example, if you're writing a function that accepts either a string or a number, it can be defined as follows:

```typescript
```

```typescript
function printValue(value: string | number): void {
console.log(value);

}
```

Here, the `printValue` function will accept either a `string` or a `number`. If you try to pass any other type, TypeScript will raise a compile-time error, ensuring that only valid types are passed.

Practical Use Case for Union Types

Consider a scenario where you're building a simple application that handles user input. You may want to accept either a username (string) or an ID (number). Using union types helps you enforce this requirement effectively.

```typescript
type UserIdentifier = string | number;

function getUserInfo(identifier: UserIdentifier): void { if (typeof identifier === 'string') {

console.log(`Fetching user information for username: ${identifier}`);

} else {

console.log(`Fetching user information for user ID: ${identifier}`);

}

}
```

With the above function, TypeScript allows you to differentiate between the handling of strings and numbers, leading to safer code and fewer runtime errors.

Exploring Literal Types

Literal types in TypeScript allow you to specify exact values as types. This feature enhances type safety by restricting variables to specific string, number, or boolean values.

Defining Literal Types

You can define a literal type using string or number values. For example:

```typescript
type Fruit = 'apple' | 'banana' | 'orange';
```

Here, the `Fruit` type can only hold one of the specified values. Any value outside of this will trigger a TypeScript error.

Using Literal Types in Functions

Literal types can be particularly useful when creating functions where you want to limit the acceptable string values. Let's consider a function that logs different messages based on the type of fruit:

```typescript
function getFruitMessage(fruit: Fruit): string { switch (fruit) {

case 'apple':

return "Apples are red or green."; case 'banana':
```

```
return "Bananas are yellow."; case 'orange':

return "Oranges are orange."; default:

return "Unknown fruit.";

}

}
```
```

The `getFruitMessage` function will only accept one of the specified fruit values. If an invalid value is passed, TypeScript will raise an error, preventing potential bugs.

## Combining Union and Literal Types

The true power of TypeScript comes when you combine union and literal types. This allows you to create complex data structures that maintain type safety throughout your application.

### Example of Combined Types

Suppose you're working on a task management application where each task can have a status that can only be either "pending," "completed," or "in-progress." You can define the status as follows:

```typescript
type TaskStatus = 'pending' | 'completed' | 'in-progress';

interface Task { title: string;

status: TaskStatus;

}
```

```
function    updateTaskStatus(task:    Task,    status:
```
```

```
TaskStatus): void { task.status = status;
console.log(`Task "${task.title}" is now ${status}.`);
}
```
```

In this example, the `Task` interface makes use of the `TaskStatus` literal type to ensure that the status field can only contain one of the predetermined string values. The function `updateTaskStatus` further enforces this type safety by ensuring valid statuses are passed.

## Benefits of Union and Literal Types

**Improved Type Safety**: Both union and literal types help prevent runtime errors by ensuring that values adhere to the specified types during the compilation.

**Enhanced Autocompletion**: When working in an editor with TypeScript support, you get better autocompletion and hints when you choose values of union or literal types, leading to increased productivity.

**Clearer Intent**: By accurately typing variables and function parameters, your code becomes more self-documenting, making it easier for others (or future you) to understand the intended use and limitations.

**Reduced Complexity**: These types simplify code by enforcing structure and predictability, making it easier to maintain and refactor.

By leveraging these features, you can create applications that are less prone to runtime errors, easier to understand, and deliver a better experience for both developers and users. As we continue to evolve the JavaScript ecosystem, these TypeScript features will
```

become increasingly vital for maintaining high-quality, maintainable applications.

Mapped and Conditional Types for Advanced Type Manipulation

This chapter dives deep into these advanced types, exploring their syntax, use cases, and practical implications in JavaScript development.

Mapped Types

Understanding Mapped Types

Mapped types allow developers to create new types by transforming an existing type through a mapping operation. They are particularly useful when you want to derive types that share a similar structure but differ in specifics.

The general syntax for a mapped type is:

```typescript
type MappedType<T> = { [K in keyof T]: NewType;
};
```

Here, `T` is the source type, and `K` iterates over each key in `T` (obtained using the `keyof` operator).

`NewType` can be any valid type transformation applied to each property. ### Example of Mapped Types

Consider a scenario where you have a type representing

user information:

```typescript
type User = { id: number; name: string; email: string;
};
```

To create a type with all properties of `User` as optional, you can use a mapped type:

```typescript
type PartialUser = {
[K in keyof User]?: User[K];
};
```

Here, `PartialUser` has the same keys as `User`, but each property is now optional. This is akin to the built-in `Partial<T>` utility type provided by TypeScript. ### Practical Usage of Mapped Types

Beyond simply making properties optional, mapped types enable patterns like:

- **Readonly Types**: Transforming a type to have all properties as read-only.

```typescript
type ReadonlyUser = {
readonly [K in keyof User]: User[K];
};
```

- **Nullable Types**: Making all properties nullable.

```typescript
type NullableUser = {
[K in keyof User]: User[K] | null;
};
```

These transformations can be incredibly useful when creating libraries or frameworks where maintaining type integrity is crucial.

Conditional Types

Understanding Conditional Types

Conditional types provide a way to express type transformations based on conditions. They follow the syntax:

```typescript
T extends U ? X : Y
```

In this expression, if type `T` can be assigned to type `U`, then the type evaluates to `X`; otherwise, it evaluates to `Y`. This feature allows for writing types that change based on other types, significantly enhancing TypeScript's type system.

Example of Conditional Types

Consider a function that takes a value and returns a string description of that value:

```typescript
```

```typescript
type ValueType<T> = T extends number ? 'number' : T extends string ? 'string' : 'unknown';
```

Here, `ValueType` checks the type of `T`. If `T` is a `number`, it returns `'number'`. If it's a `string`, it returns `'string'`. For any other type, it returns `'unknown'`.

Practical Usage of Conditional Types

Conditional types are particularly effective for type inference and enforcing constraints in function definitions. For instance, you can use them to create helper types that change behavior based on the provided type:

```typescript
type ElementType<T> = T extends (infer U)[] ? U : T;


type NumberArray = ElementType<number[]>;  // NumberArray is now number type StringType = ElementType<string>;    // StringType is still string
```

In this example, `ElementType` checks if `T` is an array. If it is, it extracts the element type; otherwise, it retains the original type.

Combining Mapped and Conditional Types

One of the most powerful aspects of TypeScript is the ability to combine mapped and conditional types. By doing this, you can create dynamic and context-sensitive types. For example:

93

```typescript
type ArrayOfTypes<T> = {
[K in keyof T]: T[K] extends string ? number : T[K];
};
type Data = { name: string; age: number;
isActive: boolean;
};
type Result = ArrayOfTypes<Data>;
// Result is { name: number; age: number; isActive:
boolean }
```

In this example, `ArrayOfTypes` transforms the `Data`
type. The `name` property changes from `string` to
`number`, while the other types remain unchanged.

Best Practices for Using Mapped and Conditional Types

Clarity: Keep your type transformations
straightforward. Complex types can lead to hard-to-read
code.

Reuse Utility Types: Utilize TypeScript's built-in
utility types (`Pick`, `Omit`, `Partial`, etc.) before
creating your own. This improves compatibility and
reduces duplication.

Documentation: Document the purpose of complex
types, especially when they involve conditional logic or

deep mappings to enhance maintainability for future developers.

Testing: Ensure your types behave as expected in various scenarios. TypeScript's compiler offers excellent feedback on type errors, so leverage this during your development process.

By mastering these advanced types, you can enhance your TypeScript development skills, leading to improved code quality, maintainability, and developer productivity. As you continue your journey with TypeScript, consider how mapped and conditional types can be leveraged to address complex problems in your applications.

Chapter 7: Object-Oriented Programming in TypeScript

Object-Oriented Programming (OOP) is a programming paradigm that uses "objects" to design applications and software. An object is a self-contained unit that contains data (attributes) and functions (methods) that operate on that data. OOP is built around several key concepts, including encapsulation, inheritance, and polymorphism. TypeScript, a superset of JavaScript, adds static typing and enhances the capabilities of OOP, making it easier to create and maintain large-scale applications.

In this chapter, we will explore how to leverage the features of TypeScript to implement OOP concepts effectively. We'll guide you through the fundamental constructs of OOP in TypeScript, including classes, interfaces, inheritance, and decorators.

7.1 Basics of Classes

In TypeScript, classes are defined using the `class` keyword. A class serves as a blueprint for creating objects and provides a structured way to group related data and functionality.

Example: Creating a Simple Class

```typescript
class Animal {

name: string;

constructor(name: string) { this.name = name;

}

speak(): void {

console.log(`${this.name} makes a noise.`);
```

```
}
}
const dog = new Animal('Dog'); dog.speak(); // Output:
Dog makes a noise.
```

In the example above, we defined a class `Animal` with a property `name` and a method `speak`. The constructor is a special method invoked when a new instance of the class is created.

7.1.1 Access Modifiers

TypeScript supports three access modifiers: `public`, `private`, and `protected`. By default, properties and methods are public, meaning they can be accessed from outside the class. Here is how to use the access modifiers:

```typescript
class Person {

private age: number; public name: string;


constructor(name: string, age: number) { this.name = name;

this.age = age;
}
public displayInfo(): void {

console.log(`Name: ${this.name}, Age: ${this.age}`);
}
private incrementAge(): void { this.age += 1;
}
```

```
}
```

```
const john = new Person('John', 30); john.displayInfo();
// Output: Name: John, Age: 30
```

```
// john.incrementAge(); // Error: Property
'incrementAge' is private.
```
```

## 7.2 Interfaces

Interfaces in TypeScript allow you to define a contract for classes. They specify the structure of an object but do not provide implementations. This allows for flexibility and the ability to implement multiple interfaces.

### Example: Defining and Implementing an Interface

```typescript
```typescript interface Shape {
area: number; calculateArea(): number;
}
class Circle implements Shape { public radius: number;
area: number;
constructor(radius: number) { this.radius = radius;
this.area = this.calculateArea();
}
calculateArea(): number {
return Math.PI * this.radius * this.radius;
}
}
const circle = new Circle(5);
```

```
console.log(`Circle Area: ${circle.area}`); // Output:
Circle Area: 78.53981633974483
```

In the example above, we defined a `Shape` interface and implemented it in the `Circle` class, demonstrating how interfaces can define a structure for classes to follow.

7.3 Inheritance

Inheritance allows a class (subclass) to inherit properties and methods from another class (superclass). This promotes code reusability and establishes a relationship between the classes.

Example: Inheriting from a Base Class

```typescript
class Dog extends Animal { constructor(name: string) {
super(name); // Call the constructor of the superclass
}
speak(): void { console.log(`${this.name} barks.`);
}
}
const myDog = new Dog('Rover'); myDog.speak(); //
Output: Rover barks.
```

In this example, `Dog` is a subclass of `Animal`. The `speak` method is overridden to provide specific functionality for the `Dog` class.

7.4 Polymorphism

Polymorphism allows methods to perform differently based on the object that it is invoked on. In TypeScript, this can be achieved through method overriding (as illustrated in the previous section) and through the use of interfaces.

Example: Polymorphic Behavior

```typescript
function makeAnimalSpeak(animal: Animal): void {
animal.speak();
}

const myAnimal: Animal = new Animal('Generic Animal');
const myDog2: Dog = new Dog('Buddy');

makeAnimalSpeak(myAnimal); // Output: Generic Animal makes a noise. makeAnimalSpeak(myDog2); // Output: Buddy barks.
```

The `makeAnimalSpeak` function demonstrates polymorphism. It can accept any subclass of `Animal`, calling the appropriate `speak` method depending on the actual instance.

7.5 Abstract Classes

Abstract classes cannot be instantiated directly and are intended to be extended by subclasses. Abstract classes can include abstract methods, which must be implemented by derived classes.

Example: Defining an Abstract Class

```typescript
abstract class Vehicle {

abstract numberOfWheels(): number;
start(): void { console.log('Vehicle started.');
}
}
class Bike extends Vehicle { numberOfWheels(): number {
return 2;
}
}
const myBike = new Bike(); myBike.start(); // Output:
Vehicle started.
console.log(`Bike has ${myBike.numberOfWheels()}
wheels.`); // Output: Bike has 2 wheels.
```

In the above example, the `Vehicle` class is abstract and contains an abstract method `numberOfWheels`, which must be implemented by any subclass, such as `Bike`.

7.6 Decorators

TypeScript also supports decorators, which enable adding metadata to classes and methods. Decorators are functions prefixed with an `@` symbol and can be used to modify class behavior or add additional functionalities.

Example: Using a Class Decorator

```typescript
function        LogClass(target:        Function)        {
console.log(`Logging: ${target.name}`);
}
@LogClass
class Cat extends Animal { speak(): void {
console.log(`${this.name} meows.`);
}
}
const myCat = new Cat('Whiskers'); myCat.speak(); //
Output: Whiskers meows.
```

The `LogClass` decorator is applied to the `Cat` class, logging the class name when it is defined. In this chapter, we have explored various essential OOP concepts in TypeScript, including classes,

interfaces, inheritance, polymorphism, abstract classes, and decorators. Understanding these concepts will enable you to design applications that are more modular, maintainable, and scalable.

Classes, Inheritance, and Access Modifiers (public, private, protected)

TypeScript, a superset of JavaScript, enhances the capabilities of JavaScript by introducing strong typing, interfaces, and several OOP features, including classes and inheritance.

This chapter will delve into TypeScript's implementation of classes and inheritance, while also unpacking the significance of access modifiers: public, private, and protected. By the end of this chapter, you will understand how to create reusable, maintainable, and encapsulated code in TypeScript, leveraging its unique features.

Understanding Classes in TypeScript

A class is a blueprint for creating objects. It encapsulates data for the object and methods to manipulate that data. In TypeScript, defining a class is straightforward. Below is an example of a simple class definition:

```typescript
class Animal {

name: string;

constructor(name: string) { this.name = name;

}

speak(): void {

console.log(`${this.name} makes a noise.`);

}

}
```

Key Elements of the Example:

Class Declaration: The keyword `class` is followed by the class name (`Animal`).

Properties: `name` is defined as a property of the `Animal` class, with its type declared as `string`.

Constructor: The `constructor` method initializes the

103

class properties. It's invoked when a new instance of the class is created.

Methods: The `speak()` method logs a message to the console, demonstrating the behavior of the

`Animal` class.

Instantiating Classes

Creating an instance of a class is easily done using the `new` keyword:

```typescript
const dog = new Animal("Dog"); dog.speak(); // Output: Dog makes a noise.
```

Inheritance in TypeScript

Inheritance allows one class to inherit the properties and methods of another class. This promotes code reusability and establishes a hierarchical relationship between classes. In TypeScript, this is achieved using the `extends` keyword.

Example of Inheritance

Let's create a subclass called `Dog` that inherits from the `Animal` class:

```typescript
class Dog extends Animal { speak(): void {
console.log(`${this.name} barks.`);
}
```

```
}
const myDog = new Dog("Buddy"); myDog.speak(); //
Output: Buddy barks.
```

Key Elements of Inheritance:

Subclassing: The `Dog` class extends the `Animal` class, inheriting its properties and methods.

Overriding Methods: The `speak()` method in `Dog` overrides the method in `Animal`, demonstrating polymorphism.

Access Modifiers: public, private, protected

TypeScript introduces access modifiers to manage visibility and accessibility of class members (properties and methods). Access modifiers help encapsulate the class's internal workings, exposing only what is necessary.

1. Public

Members declared as `public` can be accessed from anywhere in the code. By default, all class members in TypeScript are public if no access modifier is specified.

```typescript
class Person {
public name: string;
constructor(name: string) { this.name = name;
}
public greet(): void {
console.log(`Hello, my name is ${this.name}.`);
}
```

```
}
const person = new Person("Alice"); person.greet(); //
Output: Hello, my name is Alice.
```

2. Private

Members defined as `private` cannot be accessed from outside the class. This encapsulation is crucial for protecting the integrity of class internals.

```typescript
class BankAccount { private balance: number;

constructor(initialBalance: number) { this.balance =
initialBalance;
}

public deposit(amount: number): void { this.balance +=
amount;
}

public getBalance(): number { return this.balance;
}
}
const account = new BankAccount(1000);
account.deposit(500); console.log(account.getBalance());
// Output: 1500

// console.log(account.balance); // Error: Property
'balance' is private and only accessible within class
'BankAccount'.
```

```
```

3. Protected

Members declared as `protected` can be accessed within the class itself and from subclasses. This is useful for building class hierarchies where derived classes need access to certain members of the base class but should not expose them publicly.

```typescript
class Animal {
protected sound: string;
constructor(sound: string) { this.sound = sound;
}
}
class Cat extends Animal { public makeSound(): void {
console.log(`The cat says: ${this.sound}`);
}
}
const myCat = new Cat("Meow"); myCat.makeSound(); // Output: The cat says: Meow
// console.log(myCat.sound); // Error: Property 'sound' is protected and only accessible within class 'Animal' and its subclasses.
```

We explored the fundamentals of classes and inheritance in TypeScript, emphasizing how these features facilitate the organization and reuse of code. Access modifiers—public, private, and protected—play a crucial role in encapsulation, allowing developers to manage data visibility and maintain strict boundaries between external usage and internal implementation.

Abstract Classes vs Interfaces

This chapter aims to dissect these two constructs, highlighting their differences, use cases, and best practices when developing applications with TypeScript, particularly in the context of JavaScript.

1. Understanding the Basics ### 1.1 What is an Abstract Class?

An abstract class in TypeScript is a class that cannot be instantiated directly and is intended to serve as a base class for other classes. It can contain both implemented methods and abstract methods that do not have a body. The derived classes must provide an implementation for these abstract methods.

Example of an Abstract Class:

```typescript
abstract class Animal {

abstract makeSound(): void; // Abstract method

move(): void { // Concrete method
console.log("Moving...");
```

```
    }
}
class Dog extends Animal { makeSound(): void {
console.log("Woof!");
    }
}
const dog = new Dog(); dog.makeSound(); // Outputs:
Woof! dog.move(); // Outputs: Moving...
```

1.2 What is an Interface?

An interface is a contract that defines the structure of an object in TypeScript. It allows you to specify what properties and methods an object must have, without providing any implementation. Unlike abstract classes, interfaces do not provide any concrete methods.

Example of an Interface:

```typescript
interface Animal {
makeSound(): void; // Method signature move(): void; //
Method signature
}
class Dog implements Animal { makeSound(): void {

console.log("Woof!");
}
move(): void { console.log("Moving...");
```

```
}
}
```

```typescript
const dog: Animal = new Dog(); dog.makeSound(); //
Outputs: Woof! dog.move(); // Outputs: Moving...
```

2. Key Differences ### 2.1 Instantiation

Abstract Class: Cannot be instantiated directly. It serves as a blueprint for other classes.

Interface: Also cannot be instantiated, but it defines a contract that other classes must follow. ### 2.2 Implementation

Abstract Class: Can contain both abstract and concrete methods. This allows for shared functionality among derived classes.

Interface: Contains only method signatures with no implementation. It defines a guaranteed structure without sharing behavior.

2.3 Inheritance and Multiple Implementations

Abstract Class: Supports inheritance through a single base class.

Interface: Supports multiple interface implementations, allowing a class to adhere to multiple contracts.

Example of Multiple Implementations:

```typescript
interface Flyer {
```

```
fly(): void;
}
interface Swimmer { swim(): void;
}
class Duck implements Flyer, Swimmer { fly(): void {
console.log("Flying...");
}
swim(): void { console.log("Swimming...");
}
}
const duck = new Duck(); duck.fly(); // Outputs: Flying...
duck.swim(); // Outputs: Swimming...
```
```

## 3. Use Cases

### 3.1 When to Use Abstract Classes

When you want to create a base class with shared implementation that multiple classes can inherit from.

When you need to define some common behavior and also require certain methods to be implemented by subclasses.

### 3.2 When to Use Interfaces

When you want to define an API or contract that can be implemented by various classes, which may not share a common base class.

When you want to promote loose coupling in your application design by specifying what methods can be
```

called without dictating how they must be implemented.

4. Best Practices

4.1 Favor Interfaces for Type Definitions

Whenever possible, using interfaces to define the shape of data or behavior can lead to more flexible and maintainable code. Interfaces can promote better design patterns, particularly in large codebases.

4.2 Use Abstract Classes for Sharing Code

If you find yourself needing to duplicate code across multiple classes, consider using an abstract class to encapsulate shared behavior while still enforcing a contract.

Both abstract classes and interfaces play vital roles in TypeScript's type system, allowing developers to create robust applications that are easy to maintain and extend. By understanding their distinctions and knowing when to use each, developers can leverage the power of TypeScript to write cleaner, more efficient code that bridges the gap between TypeScript's strong typing and JavaScript's flexible nature.

Chapter 8: Handling Arrays, Tuples, and Enums Effectively

In this chapter, we'll explore how to handle arrays, tuples, and enums in TypeScript, discussing their unique features and how they can enhance the robustness of your applications.

8.1 Understanding Arrays in TypeScript ### 8.1.1 Defining Arrays

In TypeScript, arrays can be defined using either the array notation or the generic Array type. The array notation uses square brackets (`[]`), while the generic type utilizes the `Array<type>` syntax.

```typescript
let numbers: number[] = [1, 2, 3, 4];

let fruits: Array<string> = ['apple', 'banana', 'cherry'];
```

8.1.2 Type Safety with Arrays

One of the primary advantages of TypeScript is its type safety. If you attempt to push an incorrect type into an array, TypeScript will throw an error at compile time.

```typescript
// This will cause an error

numbers.push('string'); // Error: Argument of type 'string' is not assignable to parameter of type 'number'.
```

```
```

8.1.3 Array Methods

TypeScript extends JavaScript array methods, allowing developers to work with collections more concisely. Leveraging type annotations, you can ensure that the data returned by these methods is consistent with your expectations.

```typescript
const squaredNumbers: number[] = numbers.map(num => num * num);
```

8.1.4 Multi-dimensional Arrays

TypeScript also supports multi-dimensional arrays, providing strong typing for more complex data structures.

```typescript
let matrix: number[][] = [ [1, 2, 3],
[4, 5, 6],
[7, 8, 9]
];
```

8.2 Working with Tuples ### 8.2.1 What are Tuples?

Tuples are a special type of array that enable you to store a fixed number of elements with specified types. This can be particularly useful when you want to represent a record with diverse data types.

```typescript
```

```typescript
let person: [string, number] = ['Alice', 30];
```

8.2.2 Accessing Tuple Elements

You can access tuple elements using standard array indexing. TypeScript retains the defined types for individual elements.

```typescript
let name: string = person[0]; // Alice let age: number = person[1]; // 30
```

8.2.3 Destructuring Tuples

Destructuring provides a concise way to access tuple values, allowing developers to assign values to variables directly.

```typescript
const [name, age] = person;
```

8.2.4 Multi-type Tuples

You can define tuples with varying types to model more complex data structures, giving you the flexibility to handle diverse inputs.

```typescript
let mixedTuple: [string, boolean, number] = ['John', true, 25];
```

8.3 Enums: A Powerful Tool for Managing Constants

115

8.3.1 Defining Enums

Enums are a feature in TypeScript that allows you to define a set of named constants. They can be numeric or string-based, improving code readability and maintainability.

```typescript
typescript enum Direction {

Up, Down, Left, Right

}

enum HttpStatus { OK = 200,

NotFound = 404,

InternalServerError = 500

}
```

8.3.2 Using Enums

Once defined, enums can be used wherever a constant value is needed, thereby enhancing both legibility and the potential for code refactoring.

```typescript
function move(direction: Direction) { switch (direction) {

case Direction.Up: console.log("Moving Up"); break;

case Direction.Down: console.log("Moving Down"); break;

// additional cases...

}

}
```

8.3.3 String Enums

String enums provide a way to explicitly define string constants, making code easier to understand and manage, particularly when debugging.

```typescript
enum LogLevel {

Debug = "DEBUG", Info = "INFO", Warn = "WARN",

Error = "ERROR"

}
```

8.3.4 Heterogeneous Enums

While it's generally not recommended, TypeScript allows enums to have both string and numeric members, paving the way for unique scenarios.

```typescript
enum Response {

No = 0,

Yes = "YES"

}
```

8.4 Integrating Arrays, Tuples, and Enums

In a TypeScript application, you frequently see arrays, tuples, and enums used together to create structured and type-safe data models. For instance, you might use an array of tuples to represent a list of product items, where each tuple contains a product name, price, and availability status represented by an enum.

117

```typescript
enum Availability { InStock, OutOfStock
}

type Product = [string, number, Availability]; let products:
Product[] = [

['Laptop', 999.99, Availability.InStock],

['Smartphone', 499.99, Availability.OutOfStock],

];

// Accessing a product's information for (const product of
products) {

const [name, price, availability] = product;

console.log(`${name}:    $${price}    -    Availability:
${Availability[availability]}`);

}
```

By understanding their structures and uses within the
language, you can write cleaner, more maintainable, and
type-safe code. As you continue your journey with
TypeScript, these fundamental data types will empower
you to create applications that not only meet business
requirements but also adhere to best practices in software
development. Understanding and utilizing these features
will enhance your productivity and ensure your codebase
remains resilient in a dynamic environment.

Typed Arrays and Tuples for More Predictable Data Structures

While the dynamic nature of JavaScript allows for rapid development, it can also lead to unpredictable behaviors and bugs due to the lack of strict typing. This challenge can be addressed through the utilization of TypeScript, Microsoft's strongly typed superset of JavaScript. In this chapter, we delve into two powerful features of TypeScript: Typed Arrays and Tuples. These features not only bring predictability to data structures but also enhance performance and maintainability in your applications.

Understanding Typed Arrays ### What are Typed Arrays?

Typed Arrays are array-like objects that provide a mechanism to read and write raw binary data in memory buffers. While regular arrays in JavaScript can hold any type of data, Typed Arrays are designed to store arrays of numbers. They are particularly useful for handling binary data in web applications, especially in instances that require performance-intensive operations, such as graphics processing with WebGL or audio processing.

The generic types offered by Typed Arrays include:

`Int8Array`

`Uint8Array`

`Uint8ClampedArray`

`Int16Array`

`Uint16Array`

`Int32Array`

`Uint32Array`

`Float32Array`

`Float64Array`

Advantages of Using Typed Arrays

Performance: Typed Arrays provide better performance by allowing JavaScript engines to optimize memory usage and data access patterns. Since they are fixed in size and type, operations on Typed Arrays can significantly speed up calculations, particularly in performance-critical applications.

Memory Management: Typed Arrays allocate a continuous block of memory, enhancing data locality and cache performance. This benefit is particularly advantageous when handling large datasets.

Type Safety: Using Typed Arrays in TypeScript enforces type-checking during compilation. This means that potential errors can be caught early in the development process rather than at runtime, leading to cleaner and more reliable code.

Example of Typed Arrays in TypeScript

Let's look at a practical example of how to use Typed Arrays in TypeScript:

```typescript
// Create a Float32Array of 5 elements

const floatArray = new Float32Array(5);
```

```
// Initialize the array values floatArray.set([1.0, 2.0, 3.0, 4.0, 5.0]);
// Accessing values and performing operations for (let i = 0; i < floatArray.length; i++) {
floatArray[i] *= 2; // Doubling each value
}
// Output the resulting array
console.log(floatArray); // Output: Float32Array(5) [2, 4, 6, 8, 10]
```
```

In this example, we create a `Float32Array`, initialize it with values, perform a simple operation on each element, and finally output the results. Such operations are more efficient than regular arrays, especially with large data sets.

## Tuples: A Structured Way to Handle Mixed Data ### What are Tuples?

tuples in TypeScript are a powerful feature that allows for the creation of arrays with fixed sizes and known types for each element. Unlike regular arrays, where all elements can be of any type, tuples enforce a specific order and type for each item.

### Advantages of Using Tuples

**Type Safety**: Tuples provide stricter type-checking, ensuring that each position in the tuple contains the expected data type. This eliminates the errors often seen with arrays that can hold multiple types.

**Flexibility**: Tuples allow developers to create complex
```

data structures that can represent heterogeneous data types in a predictable manner. This is useful in scenarios where you might want to return multiple values from a function.

Destructuring: Tuples make destructuring more intuitive, allowing for easy assignment of values to variables.

Example of Tuples in TypeScript

Let's look at an example of how tuples can be utilized within TypeScript:

```typescript
// Define a tuple representing a user type User = [string, number, boolean];

// Create a user tuple

const user: User = ['Alice', 30, true];

// Accessing tuple values

const [name, age, isActive] = user;

console.log(`Name: ${name}, Age: ${age}, Active: ${isActive}`); // Name: Alice, Age: 30, Active: true


// Using a function that returns a tuple function getUserInfo(): User {

return ['Bob', 25, false];

}

const bob = getUserInfo();

console.log(bob); // Output: ['Bob', 25, false]
```

```
```

In this example, we defined a tuple `User` that consists of a string, a number, and a boolean. By using tuples, we can enforce that the user information is structured and predictable, avoiding potential issues that can arise with regular arrays.

Combining Typed Arrays and Tuples

While Typed Arrays and tuples serve different purposes, they can also complement each other in a TypeScript project. For example, you might create a tuple representing a graphical object that holds a Typed Array for the object's vertex data.

```typescript
// Define a tuple for a graphical object
type GraphicObject = [string, Float32Array];

// Create a graphic object with a name and vertex data
const squareVertices: Float32Array = new Float32Array([

-1, -1,

1, -1,

-1, 1,

1, 1

]);

const squareObject: GraphicObject = ['Square', squareVertices];

// Accessing the tuple

const [name, vertexData] = squareObject;
```

```
console.log(name); // Output: Square
console.log(vertexData); // Output: Float32Array(8) [-1,-
1,1,-1,-1,1,1,1]
```
```

Here, we define a tuple `GraphicObject` that holds the name of a graphical object and its vertex data in a

`Float32Array`. This combination allows for a clean and predictable way of handling complex data structures that require both type safety and performance.

By using these structures, you can create more predictable and maintainable JavaScript applications while leveraging the powerful features of TypeScript. As you explore more complex data interactions in your applications, remember the robustness that Typed Arrays and Tuples can contribute to your development process. With them, you not only enhance the reliability of your code but also make it easier to understand and manage.

## Leveraging Enums to Write More Readable Code

In this chapter, we will delve into Enums in TypeScript and explore how they can be utilized to write cleaner, more understandable code for projects intended for JavaScript environments.

## Understanding Enums

Enums, short for enumerations, serve as a way to define a set of named constants. This feature enables developers to create a more meaningful context rather than relying on arbitrary strings or numbers. By organizing related constants under a single umbrella, Enums enhance clarity
```

and reduce the likelihood of errors due to miscommunication or mistyping.

Basic Syntax of Enums

The syntax for defining an Enum in TypeScript is straightforward:

```typescript
enum Direction {
Up, Down, Left, Right
}
```

In this example, we have defined an Enum called `Direction`, which contains four possible values that represent the cardinal directions. Each value is assigned a numeric value starting from zero by default, but we can explicitly set these values as well:

```typescript
enum Direction {
Up = 1,
Down = 2,
Left = 3,
Right = 4
}
```

Using Enums in Code

Using Enums in our code can significantly improve readability. For instance, consider a scenario where we need to implement a functionality that processes user input for direction:

```typescript
function moveCharacter(direction: Direction) { switch
(direction) {

case Direction.Up: console.log("Moving up!"); break;

case Direction.Down: console.log("Moving down!");

break;

case Direction.Left: console.log("Moving left!"); break;

case Direction.Right: console.log("Moving right!"); break;

default:

console.log("Invalid direction!"); break;

}

}
```

In the example above, Enums provide semantic meanings to the directions rather than using magic numbers or strings (like "up" or "down"), which can lead to misinterpretation and bugs. As a developer, understanding the code becomes easier, since the intention behind each value is clear.

Benefits of Using Enums ### 1. Enhanced Readability

Enums make code more self-explanatory. Instead of guessing what a numeric value (e.g., 0, 1, 2) corresponds to, developers can quickly comprehend that `Direction.Up` means moving upward. This clarity is especially valuable in complex applications where various constants interact.

2. Reduced Errors

Using Enums minimizes potential errors caused by typos. For example, if a developer accidentally miswrites a string such as "Up" as "upwards," it leads to runtime errors that can be tedious to debug. Enums enforce type checks at compile time, ensuring only valid values are used.

3. Centralized Management of Constants

Enums group related constants together. When you need to modify the values, you can do so from a single location without hunting through the entire codebase. This centralized management often leads to fewer mistakes and less redundant code.

4. Type Safety

TypeScript Enums add a layer of type safety that JavaScript lacks. If you attempt to pass an invalid constant to a function, TypeScript will throw a compile-time error. This safeguards against many common pitfalls that occur in dynamically typed languages.

Real-World Example: User Roles in an Application

Consider a web application where users can have different roles such as Admin, Editor, and Viewer. Using Enums can help in managing these roles efficiently:

```typescript
enum UserRole {
Admin = "ADMIN",
Editor = "EDITOR", Viewer = "VIEWER"
```

```
}
function authorizeUser(role: UserRole) { switch (role) {
case UserRole.Admin: console.log("User is an Admin.");
// Grant full access break;
case UserRole.Editor: console.log("User is an Editor.");
// Grant edit access break;
case UserRole.Viewer: console.log("User is a Viewer.");
// Grant view access break;
default:
console.log("Invalid role!"); break;
}
}
// Example usages authorizeUser(UserRole.Admin);
authorizeUser(UserRole.Viewer);
```

In this code snippet, the `UserRole` Enum categorizes user roles. The `authorizeUser` function leverages the Enum to provide specific feedback based on the role, improving overall code quality.

Integrating Enums with JavaScript

TypeScript compiles down to clean JavaScript. When you use Enums, the TypeScript compiler transpiles them into an object in JavaScript that retains their structure and names, enabling seamless integration within JavaScript frameworks and libraries.

For instance, the `Direction` Enum would be converted

into an object like this:

```javascript
var Direction;
(function (Direction) {
    Direction[Direction["Up"] = 0] = "Up";
    Direction[Direction["Down"] = 1] = "Down";
    Direction[Direction["Left"] = 2] = "Left";
    Direction[Direction["Right"] = 3] = "Right";
})(Direction || (Direction = {}));
```

This object can be consumed by any JavaScript code, ensuring the functional behavior remains intact while benefiting from the improved readability and structure provided by TypeScript Enums.

By grouping related constants, providing type safety, and ensuring clarity, Enums serve as a critical tool in a TypeScript developer's arsenal. As you transition from JavaScript to TypeScript, embracing Enums not only enhances your coding practices but also paves the way for creating robust and scalable applications.

Chapter 9: Mastering Type Guards and Advanced Type Safety

One of the core features contributing to this enhanced type safety is the concept of type guards. In this chapter, we'll explore type guards in depth, focusing on how they can streamline your code and facilitate better safety measures without sacrificing the dynamic spirit of JavaScript.

9.1 Understanding Type Guards

Type guards are TypeScript constructs that allow you to narrow down the type of a variable within a conditional block. Instead of relying solely on explicit type annotations, type guards help TypeScript understand your code's logic more effectively, enabling safer and more predictable execution paths.

9.1.1 Basic Type Guards

The simplest form of type guards is using the `typeof` operator. This operator checks the type of a variable and can be particularly useful for discriminating between primitive types.

```typescript
function getLength(value: string | number): number { if (typeof value === "string") {

return value.length;

} else {

return value.toString().length;

}
```

```
}
```

In this example, the `getLength` function accepts either a string or a number. Using the `typeof` operator, we can determine which type is passed in and compute the length accordingly.

9.1.2 Instanceof Operator

For object types, the `instanceof` operator provides a way to check whether an object is an instance of a specific class or constructor function.

```typescript
class Dog { bark() {

console.log("Woof!");

}
}

class Cat { meow() {

console.log("Meow!");

}
}

function makeSound(animal: Dog | Cat) { if (animal instanceof Dog) {

animal.bark();

} else {

animal.meow();

}
}
```

```
```

In the `makeSound` function, we differentiate between `Dog` and `Cat` instances using `instanceof`, allowing us to call the appropriate method without any type-related errors.

9.2 Custom Type Guards

TypeScript allows you to define your own type guard functions. These are particularly useful when working with custom data structures or complex types. A custom type guard function is a function whose return type is a type predicate, a special return type that informs TypeScript about which type a variable is restricted to.

```typescript
interface Fish {

swim: () => void;

}

interface Bird { fly: () => void;

}

function isFish(animal: Fish | Bird): animal is Fish {
return (animal as Fish).swim !== undefined;

}

function handleAnimal(animal: Fish | Bird) { if
(isFish(animal)) {

animal.swim();

} else {

animal.fly();

}
```

```
}
```
```
```

The `isFish` function is a custom type guard that checks if the `swim` method exists on the given `animal` variable. This function narrows down the type of `animal`, enhancing safety in the `handleAnimal` function.

9.3 Using Discriminated Unions

Discriminated unions, or tagged unions, are another powerful feature in TypeScript that work seamlessly with type guards. By combining union types with a common property, you can easily narrow down types within your code.

```typescript
interface Square {
```
```
kind: "square"; size: number;
```
```
}
```
```
interface Circle { kind: "circle"; radius: number;
```
```
}
```
```
type Shape = Square | Circle;
```
```
function area(shape: Shape): number { switch (shape.kind) {
```
```
case "square":
```
```
return shape.size * shape.size; case "circle":
```
```
return Math.PI * shape.radius * shape.radius;
```
```
}
```
```
}
```
```
```

In this example, each shape has a `kind` property, allowing a straightforward switch case that effectively narrows down the type of `shape`. TypeScript's control flow analysis ensures that you only access properties relevant to the specific shape type.

9.4 Advanced Concepts in Type Safety ### 9.4.1 Type Assertions

While type guards help TypeScript infer types more accurately, there might be scenarios where you know the type better than the compiler. In these instances, you can use type assertions to inform TypeScript explicitly about the type of a variable.

```typescript
const someValue: any = "this is a string";

const strLength: number = (someValue as string).length;
```

Although type assertions can be powerful, use them cautiously, as excessive use can undermine the benefits of TypeScript's type-checking capabilities.

9.4.2 Non-null Assertion Operator

Another useful feature in TypeScript is the non-null assertion operator (`!`), which helps you assert that a variable is not null or undefined when TypeScript's type-checking is being overly cautious.

```typescript
function getUserId(user: { id?: number }) {

return user.id!; // Assert that id is not null or undefined
```

```
}
```
\` \` \`

Use this operator wisely—unwanted nullish values can lead to runtime errors.

Mastering type guards and advanced type safety in TypeScript guarantees a robust foundation for building scalable and maintainable applications. By leveraging basic type guards, custom type guards, discriminated unions, and other type safety features, developers can enhance their coding experience and minimize potential issues.

As you continue your TypeScript journey, remember that the goal is not just to enforce types but also to improve clarity and reliability in your code. The more proficient you become with TypeScript's type systems, the more confident you'll feel in your ability to write high-quality, error-resistant applications.

Using typeof, instanceof, and Custom Type Guards

One of the powerful features of TypeScript is its ability to provide type guards, which are mechanisms used to determine the type of a variable at runtime. In this chapter, we'll explore how to use `typeof`, `instanceof`, and create custom type guards to effectively manage types in your TypeScript code. Understanding these mechanisms will help you write safer and more maintainable code.

1. The `typeof` Operator

The `typeof` operator is a built-in JavaScript operator that can be used in TypeScript to ascertain the type of a variable or expression. It can be particularly useful for differentiating between primitive types.

Example of Using `typeof`

```typescript
function printValue(value: number | string) { if (typeof value === 'string') {

console.log(`String: ${value}`);

} else if (typeof value === 'number') { console.log(`Number: ${value}`);

} else {

console.log("Unsupported type!");

}

}

printValue("Hello, TypeScript!"); // Output: String: Hello, TypeScript! printValue(42); // Output: Number: 42
```

In this example, the `printValue` function takes a parameter that can be either a string or a number. Using the

`typeof` operator, we check the type at runtime and handle it accordingly. ### Common Use Cases of `typeof`

Primitives: You can check for `string`, `number`, `boolean`, `undefined`, and `symbol`.

136

Function Types: You can check if a variable is a function (`typeof value === 'function'`).

Object Type: Use `typeof` to differentiate between `null`, objects, arrays, and functions. ## 2. The `instanceof` Operator

The `instanceof` operator is used to test if an object is an instance of a particular class or constructor function. This is especially useful when working with custom objects or classes.

Example of Using `instanceof`

```typescript
class Animal {
eat() {
console.log('Eating...');
}
}


class Dog extends Animal { bark() {
console.log('Woof!');
}
}
function handleAnimal(animal: Animal) { if (animal instanceof Dog) {
animal.bark(); // Safe to call bark
} else {
animal.eat(); // Safe to call eat
```

```
}
}
```

```
const myDog = new Dog(); handleAnimal(myDog); //
Output: Woof!
```
```` ``` ````

In the above example, we define a base class `Animal` and a derived class `Dog`. The `handleAnimal` function checks if the provided `animal` is an instance of `Dog` using `instanceof`, allowing us to safely call class-specific methods.

When to Use `instanceof`

When you have a hierarchy of classes and want to differentiate between them.

When dealing with constructor functions.

For complex object types where inheritance is involved.

3. Custom Type Guards

TypeScript allows you to create your own type guards, which can further assist in type narrowing. A custom type guard is a function that returns a boolean and asserts a specific type in its return type.

Creating a Custom Type Guard

```typescript
type Cat = { type: 'cat';

meow: () => void;

};

type Dog = { type: 'dog'; bark: () => void;

};
```
```

```
function isCat(animal: Cat | Dog): animal is Cat { return
animal.type === 'cat';
}
function handlePet(pet: Cat | Dog) { if (isCat(pet)) {
pet.meow(); // Safe to call meow
} else {

pet.bark(); // Safe to call bark
}
}
const myCat: Cat = { type: 'cat',
meow: () => console.log('Meow!'),
};
handlePet(myCat); // Output: Meow!
```
```

In this example, the `isCat` function is a custom type
guard that checks whether the provided `animal` is a

`Cat` based on its `type` property. The return type
`animal is Cat` informs TypeScript that if `isCat` returns

`true`, the variable `animal` should be treated as a `Cat`.
### Benefits of Custom Type Guards

**Readability**: They make your intentions clear when
checking types.

**Reusability**: Custom guards can be reused across your
codebase.
```

Type Safety: They enhance type safety and reduce the possibility of runtime errors.

In this chapter, we've explored the practical uses of `typeof`, `instanceof`, and custom type guards in TypeScript. These tools are essential for effective type management in TypeScript codebases, allowing developers to differentiate between types at runtime safely. By mastering these concepts, you can enhance the robustness and maintainability of your TypeScript applications, paving the way for a more efficient development experience.

Quick Summary

The `typeof` operator checks for primitive types and some functions.

The `instanceof` operator tests whether an object is an instance of a particular class.

Custom type guards allow you to create specific checks and enhance type narrowing.

Handling Unknown and Optional Values with unknown and optional chaining

With optional chaining, TypeScript enhances the safety and readability of our code, allowing developers to address nullable values and deep nested properties with ease.

In this chapter, we will explore how TypeScript's features—particularly optional chaining and the `unknown` type—can facilitate robust JavaScript applications. This chapter includes practical examples and best practices to ensure you can effectively manage unknown and optional values.

Understanding Unknown Values

In TypeScript, the `unknown` type is a top type, meaning it can represent any value like `any`, but with added safety. When a value is of type `unknown`, it means you cannot perform operations on it until you perform some type of checking. This encourages better handling of dynamic data structures and helps prevent runtime errors.

Example: Declaring Unknown

```typescript
let result: unknown;

result = "Hello, world!"; // Valid result = 42;     // Valid

result = true; // Valid

result = null; // Valid

result = {};    // Valid
```

Attempting to access properties on `result` would lead to an error:

```typescript
console.log(result.length); // Error: Object is of type 'unknown'.
```

141

To manipulate an `unknown` value, you need to narrow down its type using type guards:

```typescript
if (typeof result === "string") {

console.log(result.length); // Works because we checked the type.

}
```

Introducing Optional Values

In JavaScript, dealing with properties that may or may not exist is a common scenario, often leading to confusion and null reference errors. The introduction of optional properties in TypeScript helps to explicitly define this uncertainty.

Declaring Optional Properties

You can declare optional properties in an interface using the `?` modifier. This allows consumers of the interface to interact with properties safely.

```typescript interface User {

id: number; name: string;

email?: string; // Optional property

}
const user: User = { id: 1,

name: "Alice",

// email is not required
```

```
};
```

When accessing the optional property, TypeScript ensures that you handle the possibility that it could be undefined.

Optional Chaining

Optional chaining (`?.`) is a powerful feature in TypeScript/JavaScript that allows you to safely access deeply nested properties without having to check if each reference in the chain is valid.

The Syntax of Optional Chaining

```typescript
const user: User = { id: 1, name: "Bob" };

// Accessing an optional property safely

const userEmail = user.email?.toLowerCase(); // Returns
undefined if email doesn't exist
```

Without optional chaining, you would have to write cumbersome checks:

```typescript
const userEmail = user.email ? user.email.toLowerCase() :
undefined;
```

With optional chaining, the syntax becomes cleaner and more readable, significantly reducing the risk of runtime errors.

Combining Unknown, Optional, and Optional

143

Chaining

The true power of TypeScript comes from combining these features. Consider an API response whose structure is not guaranteed. Here's how to handle such a scenario using `unknown`, `optional`, and optional chaining together.

Example: Handling Unknown API Responses

```typescript
interface ApiResponse { user?: {

id: number; name: string; email?: string;

};
}
function handleApiResponse(response: unknown) { const apiResponse = response as ApiResponse;

const                     userEmail                    =
apiResponse.user?.email?.toLowerCase();
console.log(userEmail ?? "No email provided");

}
// Simulate an API response const response = {

user: {

id: 1,

name: "Charlie",

// email is missing

},
```

```
};
```

handleApiResponse(response); // Outputs: No email provided
```
` ` `
```

In this example, we safely handle an API response that could contain optional nested properties. We use optional chaining to navigate through the `user` object, preventing runtime errors while allowing for dynamic structures.

Best Practices for Handling Unknown and Optional Values

Use `unknown` instead of `any`: Leverage `unknown` for values that could be of any type but still want to enforce type checking.

Utilize Optional Properties Wisely: Use optional properties in interfaces when dealing with dynamic or partial data structures.

Adopt Optional Chaining: Embrace optional chaining for a cleaner approach to accessing nested properties. It reduces boilerplate code and the potential for null reference errors.

Type Guards: Implement type guards for `unknown` values to narrow down to specific types before using them.

Default Values: Consider using nullish coalescing (`??`) or default parameters to handle undefined values gracefully.

By using `unknown`, optional properties, and optional chaining, you'll find that your code is clearer and less prone to errors. Throughout your journey in TypeScript, embrace these tools to navigate the complexities of

145

modern JavaScript data handling confidently.

Chapter 10: Working with Modules and Namespaces

TypeScript, being a superset of JavaScript, introduces powerful tools for code organization through modules and namespaces. This chapter delves into these concepts and illustrates how they can be utilized effectively in TypeScript projects, providing a clear pathway for integrating them into JavaScript environments.

Understanding Modules ### What are Modules?

Modules are self-contained units of code that encapsulate functionality and can be easily reused across different parts of an application. In TypeScript, a module is simply a file that contains specific code, which can export parts of this code and enable other files to import it.

Basic Syntax

In TypeScript, you can define a module using the `export` keyword:

```typescript
// mathUtils.ts

export function add(a: number, b: number): number {
return a + b;
}

export function subtract(a: number, b: number): number {
return a - b;
}
```

```
```

You can then import these functions in another file:

```typescript
// main.ts

import { add, subtract } from './mathUtils';
console.log(add(5, 3)); // Outputs: 8

console.log(subtract(5, 3)); // Outputs: 2
```

Module Formats

TypeScript supports various module formats to align with JavaScript environments, including CommonJS (used in Node.js), AMD (Asynchronous Module Definition), UMD (Universal Module Definition), and ES Modules (ESM).

Example of CommonJS

If you prefer using CommonJS syntax, you can modify the module code as follows:

```typescript
// mathUtils.ts

export function add(a: number, b: number): number {
return a + b;
}

export function subtract(a: number, b: number): number {
return a - b;
}
```

```
```

And you can use it like this in Node.js:

```javascript
// main.js

const { add, subtract } = require('./mathUtils.js');
console.log(add(5, 3)); // Outputs: 8

console.log(subtract(5, 3)); // Outputs: 2
```

Namespaces in TypeScript

While modules are now the preferred way to structure code, TypeScript also provides an alternative known as namespaces (previously known as internal modules). Namespaces are primarily used to group related code in a single logical unit.

Defining a Namespace

You can create a namespace using the `namespace` keyword:

```typescript
// utility.ts

namespace StringUtilities {

export function toUpperCase(str: string): string { return str.toUpperCase();

}

export function toLowerCase(str: string): string { return str.toLowerCase();

}
```

148

```
}
```
` ` `

Using a Namespace

To access functions defined in a namespace, you simply reference it:

` ` `typescript

// main.ts

/// <reference path="utility.ts" ></reference>

console.log(StringUtilities.toUpperCase("hello"));   // Outputs: HELLO
console.log(StringUtilities.toLowerCase("WORLD")); // Outputs: world

` ` `

Comparing Modules and Namespaces

While namespaces are useful for quickly grouping related functions and types, modules offer better support for code organization in larger applications. Modern JavaScript development, aided by tools like Webpack and bundlers, strongly favors modules over namespaces. It is generally recommended to use modules in new TypeScript projects.

Practical Tips for Working with Modules

File Naming: Use descriptive file names that convey the purpose of the module.

Organize Code: Group related functionality together within a module and expose only what is necessary.

Use Barrel Files: Create a single file that re-exports modules from multiple files. This simplifies imports:

```typescript
// index.ts

export * from './mathUtils'; export * from './stringUtilities';
```

Type Definitions: Utilize `d.ts` files for providing type information for third-party libraries without TypeScript support.

The concepts of modules and namespaces in TypeScript provide developers with robust mechanisms to organize, encapsulate, and reuse code effectively. As we move further into development with TypeScript, modules should be the primary focus as they align more closely with modern JavaScript practices. By mastering these concepts, developers can create scalable, maintainable, and organized codebases, paving the way for clearer collaboration and better software architecture.

ES6 Modules and TypeScript—How to Structure Your Codebase

In this chapter, we'll explore how to leverage ES6 modules and TypeScript to craft a well-structured codebase that is not only easy to navigate but also robust and type-safe.

1. Understanding ES6 Modules ### 1.1 What are ES6 Modules?

ES6 (ECMAScript 2015) introduced a standardized

module system to JavaScript, allowing developers to break their code into separate files. This modular approach promotes reusability and better organization. A module is simply a file with a `.js` or `.ts` extension, and it can export variables, functions, classes, or objects, which can then be imported into other modules.

1.2 Importing and Exporting

The syntax for exporting a module is straightforward:

- **Named exports** allow you to export multiple values from a module:

```javascript
// utils.js
export const PI = 3.14; export function add(x, y) {
return x + y;
}
```

- **Default exports** allow you to export a single value:

```javascript
// math.js
const multiply = (x, y) => x * y; export default multiply;
```

You can then import these values in other modules:

```javascript
// app.js
import { PI, add } from './utils'; import multiply from
```

```
'./math';
```
```
` ` `
```

This clear separation of code allows for easier understanding and reuse of components. ## 2. Introduction to TypeScript

2.1 What is TypeScript?

TypeScript is a superset of JavaScript that adds optional static typing to the language. With its powerful type system, TypeScript can catch errors during compile time, allowing for a smoother debugging process and enhancing the development experience. TypeScript compiles to plain JavaScript, ensuring compatibility across all JavaScript environments.

2.2 Benefits of Using TypeScript

Static Typing: TypeScript's type system helps prevent runtime errors by catching type errors during development.

Enhanced IDE Support: Most IDEs offer better autocompletion, navigation, and refactoring features when using TypeScript.

Interfaces and Types: TypeScript allows the definition of interfaces and custom types, making your code more robust and self-documenting.

3. Structuring a TypeScript Codebase ### 3.1 Directory Structure

A well-organized directory structure is vital for maintainability. Here's a common structure for a

TypeScript project:
```

/my-project

/src

/components# Reusable UI components

/models      # Type definitions and interfaces

/services    # API calls and service logic

/utils  # Utility functions index.ts        # Entry point


/tests  # Test files


package.json        # Project metadata and dependencies
tsconfig.json  #  TypeScript  configuration  README.md
                # Project documentation
```

3.2 Utilizing Type Definitions

Defining types and interfaces is essential for a TypeScript codebase. Use interfaces to define the shape of complex objects. For instance, if you're working with a User model:

```typescript
// src/models/User.ts export interface User {

id: number; name: string; email: string;

}
```

```
` ` `
```

This provides clarity and ensures that objects conform to the expected structure throughout your application.

3.3 Module Organization

Organizing your code into logical modules enhances readability and maintainability. Ensure that each module has a single responsibility. For instance, a `UserService` module that handles user-related operations might look like this:

```typescript
// src/services/UserService.ts

import { User } from '../models/User';

class UserService {

private users: User[] = [];

addUser(user: User) { this.users.push(user);

}

getUsers(): User[] { return this.users;

}

}

export default new UserService();
```

3.4 Export and Import Best Practices

Use named exports when you want to export multiple members from a module. This makes it clear what you're importing.

Use default exports for modules that primarily export a single entity.

This promotes clarity and flexibility in managing how your code is consumed by different parts of your application.

4. Tips for a TypeScript and ES6 Module Workflow
4.1 Leverage TypeScript Configuration

The `tsconfig.json` file allows you to customize TypeScript's behavior. Key properties you might want to set include:

`target`: The version of JavaScript you want to compile to (e.g., ES6, ES2015).

`module`: Specifies the module system to use (e.g., ES6, CommonJS).

`strict`: Enables all strict type-checking options. ### 4.2 Use Type Definitions from the Community

When working with third-party libraries, you may encounter the need for type definitions. The DefinitelyTyped repository provides community-contributed type definitions. You can install them using npm with:

```bash
npm install --save-dev @types/library-name
```

By utilizing TypeScript's features like strong typing and interfaces alongside the modularity of ES6, you set the stage for a scalable application architecture. As you adopt these practices, your code will not only be easier to work with but also more resilient to changes and growth.

Leveraging TypeScript Declaration Files (.d.ts) for Third-Party Libraries

This chapter will explore how TypeScript declaration files (.d.ts) can bridge this gap, enabling developers to take full advantage of TypeScript's features while working with JavaScript libraries.

Understanding TypeScript Declaration Files

At its core, a TypeScript declaration file (.d.ts) serves as a bridge between JavaScript and TypeScript. It provides TypeScript with type information about JavaScript code, allowing developers to leverage TypeScript's static typing, autocompletion, and error-checking features. A declaration file describes the shape of a JavaScript library, detailing its functions, classes, and variables while maintaining compatibility with the underlying JavaScript code.

Why Use Declaration Files?

Type Safety: By providing type definitions, declaration files allow developers to catch errors at compile time rather than runtime, reducing the likelihood of bugs in production code.

IntelliSense Support: IDEs and text editors can offer better autocompletion, tooltips, and navigation features when they have access to type information, thus improving the overall development experience.

Documentation: Declaration files act as informal documentation, clarifying how to use functions, what parameters to pass, and what return types to expect.

Interoperability: They enable seamless integration between JavaScript libraries and TypeScript projects, making it easier to adopt TypeScript incrementally in an existing codebase.

Types of Declaration Files

Declaration files can be divided into two categories:

Global Declaration Files: These files declare types globally accessible throughout the project. They usually reside in a file named `index.d.ts` or in dedicated `.d.ts` files within a module.

Module Declaration Files: These files provide type definitions specific to particular modules or packages. A common pattern is to have a file that matches the name of the JavaScript module being used.

Creating Your Own Declaration Files

When third-party libraries do not have existing type definitions (or those available are outdated), you may need to create your own declaration file. Here's a step-by-step guide:

Identify the Library Usage: Determine the parts of the library you will use and the types you need.

Create a Declaration File: You can create a new `.d.ts` file in your project, typically in a `types` directory, naming it according to the library (e.g., `my-library.d.ts`).

Define Types: Declare the types of functions, classes, and variables you will use. Here's an example for a fictional library:

```typescript
// my-library.d.ts
declare module 'my-library' {
export function add(a: number, b: number): number;
export function subtract(a: number, b: number): number;
}
```

Reference the Declaration File: Ensure that TypeScript recognizes your declaration file by including it in the `tsconfig.json` or explicitly referencing it in your TypeScript files.

Using DefinitelyTyped

For popular libraries, there is a high chance that someone has already created comprehensive type definitions. The community-driven repository, DefinitelyTyped, is the primary source for such definitions. To use definitions from DefinitelyTyped, you can install them via npm. For example:

```bash
npm install @types/lodash
```

This commands installs the type definitions for the Lodash library, which enables you to use it with type safety in your TypeScript code.

Using Third-Party Libraries in TypeScript

After setting up the declaration files, you can easily import and use third-party libraries in your TypeScript projects. Here's how:

Importing the Library: Use the standard import syntax to include the library in your TypeScript files.

```typescript
import { add, subtract } from 'my-library';

const resultAdd = add(5, 3); // TypeScript knows the return type is number const resultSubtract = subtract(10, 4);
```

Exploiting Type Information: Take advantage of type checking and IDE features, such as hover tooltips and autocomplete functionalities, that enhance development.

Leveraging TypeScript declaration files is essential for maintaining type safety and enhancing the development experience when working with third-party JavaScript libraries. By understanding how to create and use these declaration files, developers can significantly improve their TypeScript projects' robustness and maintainability.

Chapter 11: Error Handling and Debugging in TypeScript

This chapter will delve into the intricacies of error handling, the various error types in TypeScript, and debugging strategies that help streamline the development process.

11.1 Understanding Types of Errors

Before we dive into error handling, it is crucial to understand the different types of errors you may encounter while developing applications in TypeScript:

11.1.1 Compile-Time Errors

Compile-time errors occur when the TypeScript compiler catches issues in your code before it is run. Common examples include type mismatches, syntax errors, or the use of undeclared variables. These errors are beneficial because they allow developers to correct issues before execution, improving code quality.

11.1.2 Runtime Errors

Runtime errors occur while the program is executing. These could be caused by referencing undefined variables, attempting to perform illegal operations (such as dividing by zero), or network request failures. Unlike compile-time errors, runtime errors may only become apparent during testing or real-world usage.

11.1.3 Logical Errors

Logical errors are often the most difficult to identify. These occur when the code runs without crashing, but produces incorrect results. Logical errors can stem from improper algorithm implementation, incorrect data handling, or unintentional side effects in the code.

11.2 Error Handling in TypeScript

TypeScript provides mechanisms to handle errors gracefully, allowing developers to build robust applications. Here's a closer look at how to manage errors effectively:

11.2.1 The `try...catch` Statement

Using `try...catch` blocks is a common way to catch and handle runtime errors in TypeScript. Here's how it works:

```typescript
function parseJSON(jsonString: string) { try {

const result = JSON.parse(jsonString); return result;

} catch (error) {

console.error('Invalid JSON string:', error); return null; // or handle error as appropriate

}

}

const jsonString = '{"name": "Alice", "age": 30}'; // Valid JSON const result = parseJSON(jsonString);

console.log(result);

const invalidJsonString = '{"name": "Alice", "age": '; // Invalid JSON const invalidResult = parseJSON(invalidJsonString); console.log(invalidResult);
```

In the code above, if `JSON.parse` fails, the error will be

caught in the `catch` block, allowing for error logging without crashing the application.

11.2.2 Custom Error Classes

Creating custom error classes can enhance error handling by providing more context about the error conditions. Here's an example:

```typescript
class ValidationError extends Error {
constructor(message: string) {
super(message);
this.name = 'ValidationError';
}
}
function validateUserInput(input: string) { if (!input) {
throw new ValidationError('Input cannot be empty');
}
// Further validation logic
}
try {
validateUserInput('');
} catch (error) {
if (error instanceof ValidationError) {
console.error('Validation Error:', error.message);
} else {
console.error('An unexpected error occurred:', error);
```

```
}
}
```

Custom error classes allow for more granular error management and can help in categorizing errors effectively, enhancing debugging efforts.

11.2.3 Asynchronous Error Handling

Asynchronous programming presents additional challenges concerning error handling, typically handled through promises and async/await syntax.

Using `try...catch` with async functions is a straightforward solution:

```typescript
async function fetchData(url: string): Promise<any> { try {

const response = await fetch(url); if (!response.ok) {

throw new Error(`HTTP error! status: ${response.status}`);

}

const data = await response.json(); return data;

} catch (error) {

console.error('Error fetching data:', error); throw error; // propagate the error if needed

}
}
```

```
```

In the example above, any errors thrown inside the `try` block will be caught in the `catch` block, including network errors and non-2xx HTTP responses.

11.3 Debugging in TypeScript

Debugging is an essential skill when developing applications. TypeScript provides several tools and techniques to aid in the debugging process.

11.3.1 Using Source Maps

TypeScript compiles `.ts` files to `.js`, which can make debugging difficult. Source maps bridge this gap by mapping the compiled JavaScript back to the original TypeScript code. Most modern browsers support source maps, allowing developers to set breakpoints and inspect variables in TypeScript files directly.

To enable source maps, ensure your `tsconfig.json` includes:

```json
{
"compilerOptions": { "sourceMap": true
}
}
```

11.3.2 Debugging with IDEs

Integrated Development Environments (IDEs) like Visual Studio Code provide robust debugging tools. With breakpoints, watch expressions, and call stack inspection, developers can thoroughly trace the execution of their TypeScript applications.

Set breakpoints by clicking on the left margin in the code editor.

Use the debug panel to start debugging sessions and inspect variable values. ### 11.3.3 Console Logging

While not a replacement for proper debugging tools, console logging remains a valuable technique for quickly checking the state of your code. Using `console.log()` judiciously can help trace the execution flow and uncover logical errors.

```typescript
function calculateTotal(items: number[]) { let total = 0;

items.forEach((item) => {

console.log('Adding item:', item); // Debug log total += item;

});

return total;

}

calculateTotal([10, 20, 30]);
```

By utilizing features such as the `try...catch` statement, custom error classes, and the power of modern IDEs, developers can significantly reduce the time spent on identifying and resolving issues. Armed with these tools and techniques, you are better equipped to handle errors gracefully and debug your TypeScript applications more efficiently.

Common TypeScript Errors and How to Fix Them

In this chapter, we will explore common TypeScript errors that may arise and how to resolve them effectively.

1. Type Mismatch Errors ### Description

One of the most frequent errors in TypeScript is the type mismatch error. When TypeScript's type checker

encounters an operation that involves mismatched types, it will throw an error.

Example

```typescript
let count: number = 5;

count = "five"; // Error: Type 'string' is not assignable to type 'number'.
```

Solution

Ensure that variables are assigned the correct type. In the above example, you should change the assignment to a number:

```typescript
let count: number = 5;

count = 10; // Correct assignment
```

```
```

Alternatively, you could use a union type if you genuinely need a variable to store multiple types:

```typescript
let count: number | string = 5; count = "five"; // Now allowed
```

2. Property Does Not Exist on Type ### Description

This error occurs when you try to access a property that TypeScript cannot recognize as part of the specified type.

Example

```typescript
interface User { name: string; age: number;
}

const user: User = { name: "Alice", age: 30 };

console.log(user.email); // Error: Property 'email' does not exist on type 'User'.
```

Solution

To resolve this, check the type definition to ensure that you are accessing properties that actually exist. If needed, you can extend the interface:

```typescript
interface User { name: string; age: number;

email?: string; // Optional property

}
```

```typescript
const user: User = { name: "Alice", age: 30, email: "alice@example.com" }; console.log(user.email); // Now allowed
```

3. Type 'X' is Not Assignable to Type 'Y' ### Description

This error occurs when you attempt to assign a value of a particular type to a variable that expects a different type.

Example

```typescript
let greeting: string = "Hello";

greeting = 42; // Error: Type 'number' is not assignable to type 'string'.
```

Solution

Ensure that the types are compatible. In this case, we want to ensure that only a string can be assigned to the

`greeting` variable:

```typescript
let greeting: string = "Hello";

greeting = "Hi"; // Correct assignment
```

If you need to store both strings and numbers, consider using union types:

```typescript
```

```
let greeting: string | number = "Hello"; greeting = 42; //
Now allowed
```

4. Function Doesn't Exist on Type ### Description

When calling a method on an object that doesn't exist in the object's type definition, TypeScript will generate an error.

Example

```typescript
interface Logger {

log(message: string): void;

}


const logger: Logger = {

log: message => console.log(message),

};

logger.error("This is an error"); // Error: Property 'error'
does not exist on type 'Logger'.
```

Solution

Ensure that you are calling methods that are defined within the interface. If you wish to add functionality, modify the interface:

```typescript
interface Logger {

log(message: string): void;

error(message: string): void; // Adding error method
```

```
}
const logger: Logger = {
log: message => console.log(message),
error: message => console.error(message),  // Implementing the error method
};
logger.error("This is an error"); // Now allowed
```

5. Missing Return Type in Function ### Description

TypeScript encourages explicitness, and if you don't specify the return type for a function, it will infer the type based on the return statement. However, if it cannot infer it correctly, it might lead to unexpected behavior.

Example

```typescript
function add(a, b) {
return a + b; // Error: Parameter 'a' implicitly has an 'any' type.
}
```

Solution

Explicitly define the return and parameter types for better clarity and type safety:

```typescript
function add(a: number, b: number): number { return a + b; // No errors, clear expectations
```

```
}
```

6. Any Type Usage ### Description

While the `any` type allows you to bypass type checking, its use can lead to runtime errors and defeats the purpose of TypeScript's static typing.

Example

```typescript
let data: any = "Hello";

data = 100; // Allowed, but potentially dangerous
```

Solution

Avoid using `any` and instead use specific types or generics when necessary. For example, if you need to handle multiple types, you can use a union type:

```typescript
let data: string | number = "Hello";

data = 100; // Now allowed, while still being type-safe
```

By familiarizing yourself with common TypeScript errors such as type mismatches, property access issues, and function signature checks, you can enhance your coding experience and write more robust applications. Always aim for clear type definitions, and embrace TypeScript's features to prevent errors before they reach runtime.

Debugging TypeScript Code with VS Code and Developer Tools

This chapter will explore practical techniques for debugging TypeScript code using Visual Studio Code (VS Code) and browser developer tools. By the end of this chapter, you will have the tools and techniques to diagnose and resolve issues in your TypeScript applications quickly.

1. Setting Up Your Environment ### 1.1 Installing Visual Studio Code

Before you can start debugging, ensure that you have Visual Studio Code installed. You can download it from the [official website](https://code.visualstudio.com/).

1.2 Setting Up TypeScript

If you haven't already set up a TypeScript project, you can do so by initializing a new project. Open a terminal, create a new folder for your project, and run the following commands:

```bash

mkdir my-typescript-app cd my-typescript-app npm init -y

npm install typescript --save-dev npx tsc --init

```

This will create a basic `tsconfig.json` file, which controls how TypeScript is compiled. You can modify this file to suit your project needs.

1.3 Installing the Required Extensions

To improve your debugging experience, install the following VS Code extensions:

- **Debugger for Chrome**: This extension allows you to debug JavaScript in the Chrome browser and directly in VS Code.

To install it, go to the Extensions view (`Ctrl+Shift+X`), search for "Debugger for Chrome", and click "Install".

2. Configuring Debugging in VS Code ### 2.1 Launch Configuration

To debug your TypeScript code, you need to create a launch configuration. Open the debug view in VS Code by clicking on the bug icon in the sidebar or pressing `Ctrl+Shift+D`. Click on "create a launch.json file" and select "Chrome" from the dropdown.

Here's an example configuration for debugging a TypeScript application:

```json
{
"version": "0.2.0", "configurations": [
{
"type": "chrome",
"request": "launch",
"name": "Launch Chrome against localhost", "url": "http://localhost:3000",
"webRoot": "${workspaceFolder}", "sourceMaps": true
```

```
    }
  ]
}
```

Make sure the `url` points to your development server. The `webRoot` should generally point to your project folder where your `.ts` files are located.

2.2 Running Your TypeScript Application

You'll need to compile your TypeScript code into JavaScript for it to run in the browser. In one terminal, run:

```bash
npx tsc --watch
```

In another terminal, run your web server (for example, using Express, a simple Node.js server, or any static server that serves your files).

3. Debugging Your Application ### 3.1 Setting Breakpoints

Open the TypeScript file you want to debug. Click in the gutter (the left margin) next to the line number where you want to set a breakpoint. A red dot will appear, indicating a breakpoint has been set.

3.2 Starting the Debugger

To start debugging, go back to the debug view in VS Code, select your launch configuration from the dropdown, and click the green play button (or press `F5`). This will launch Chrome and open your specified URL.

3.3 Inspecting Variables

When execution hits a breakpoint, the code execution will pause, and the debug pane will show the current call stack and current variables. You can hover over variable names to see their current values. Use the "Watch" section to keep an eye on specific variables or expressions.

3.4 Stepping Through Code

You can control the execution flow using the following options:

Step Over (F10): Executes the current line and moves to the next line in the same function.

Step Into (F11): If the current line contains a function call, this moves execution into that function.

Step Out (Shift + F11): Completes the current function and returns to the calling function. ### 3.5 Using the Debug Console

The Debug Console is an interactive console that allows you to execute expressions and interact with the application's runtime context. You can access it in the debug pane. Use it to evaluate expressions and modify variable values on-the-fly.

4. Debugging with Browser Developer Tools

When working with web applications, developer tools in browsers like Chrome provide powerful capabilities. Here's how to leverage them:

4.1 Opening Developer Tools

You can open Chrome Developer Tools by right-clicking

175

anywhere on the webpage and selecting "Inspect," or by pressing `Ctrl+Shift+I`.

4.2 Using the Sources Panel

In the Sources panel, you can find the transpiled JavaScript files and set breakpoints directly in your TypeScript code. This is particularly useful if you need to debug in an environment where VS Code's debugger is not available.

4.3 Console Logging

While debugging, simple `console.log()` statements can help you track down issues quickly. Make use of the console section in developer tools to see these logs in real-time.

4.4 Performance Analysis

The Performance tab helps you understand how your code executes. You can record a session and analyze the time taken by functions, allowing you to optimize your code performance.

5. Common Debugging Scenarios

Null or Undefined Errors: Use the "Watch" feature to keep track of specific variables that could potentially be null or undefined.

Type Mismatches: TypeScript's type checking can catch many errors at compile time, but dynamic scenarios may slip through. Use runtime checks or assertions.

API Call Issues: If you're debugging an HTTP request, inspect the Network tab in Developer Tools to see request and response details.

With practice, you'll develop a strong debugging skillset that enhances your development workflow, allowing you to create more robust TypeScript applications. Remember that debugging is not just about fixing errors; it's also about understanding your code deeply and continually improving both your code and your processes.

Conclusion

As we reach the end of this journey through TypeScript, we hope you have gained valuable insights and practical knowledge that empowers you as a JavaScript developer. Transitioning from JavaScript to TypeScript may seem daunting at first, but the benefits of adopting TypeScript are profound and far-reaching.

Throughout this guide, we have walked through the key features of TypeScript, from its strong typing system to its powerful tooling and support for modern JavaScript constructs. You should now appreciate how TypeScript not only enhances your coding experience but also contributes significantly to the creation of safer and more maintainable codebases.

Embracing TypeScript can lead to increased productivity, fewer bugs, and a smoother development process, especially in larger projects where collaboration among teams is key. By leveraging TypeScript's static typing, interfaces, and advanced features such as generics, you can write code that is not only efficient but also resilient to change.

Remember that the journey doesn't end here. The TypeScript ecosystem continues to evolve, bringing new capabilities and best practices. We encourage you to keep exploring, experimenting, and contributing to this vibrant community. Engage with other developers, share your experiences, and stay updated with the latest developments to fully harness the potential of TypeScript.

As you return to your projects, keep in mind the principles you've learned in this guide. Apply TypeScript to tackle complex logic with ease, enhance your code clarity, and ultimately deliver robust applications that meet and exceed user expectations.

Thank you for embarking on this adventure with us. We hope this book serves as a valuable resource on your path to becoming a more proficient and innovative developer. Happy coding!

Biography

Adrian Miller is a passionate technologist, web development expert, and the visionary mind behind groundbreaking digital solutions. With a deep-rooted love for **TypeScript programming, web development, and cutting-edge web applications**, Adrian has dedicated his career to transforming ideas into dynamic, high-performance digital experiences.

Driven by an insatiable curiosity and a commitment to innovation, Adrian's expertise spans across front-end and back-end development, harnessing the power of modern technologies to build scalable and efficient web applications. His ability to **simplify complex concepts and turn them into actionable insights** makes his work not only powerful but also accessible to developers and entrepreneurs alike.

Beyond coding, Adrian is an advocate for **continuous learning and sharing knowledge**, believing that the digital world thrives when creators push boundaries and explore new possibilities. Whether crafting seamless user interfaces, optimizing performance, or mentoring aspiring developers, his passion for the web shines through in every project he undertakes.

In this book, Adrian distills his **years of experience, practical know-how, and innovative mindset** into a comprehensive guide that empowers readers to **master Miller** and elevate their development skills to new heights. If you're ready to unlock your full potential in web development, you're in the right place—Adrian Miller is here to guide you on the journey.

Glossary: TypeScript for JavaScript Developers

A

Abstract Class: A class that cannot be instantiated on its own and is intended to be subclassed. It can include abstract methods that must be implemented by derived classes.

Any: A TypeScript type that allows a variable to hold values of any type. It acts as a wildcard and bypasses type checking, which can lead to runtime errors if not handled cautiously.

B

Binding: The process of connecting a variable or parameter with a specific location in memory. In TypeScript, bindings can be more specific due to its type annotations.

C

Class: A blueprint for creating objects that defines properties and methods. TypeScript supports the same class-based object-oriented programming that JavaScript does, with added features like access modifiers.

Compiler: The tool that translates TypeScript code into JavaScript. It checks for type errors and outputs clean JavaScript compatible with the specified version of ECMAScript.

D

Decorator: A special kind of declaration that can be attached to a class, method, accessor, property, or parameter to modify its behavior. Decorators can be used for logging, access control, and more.

Definition File: A file that contains type definitions for a JavaScript module. These files (with a `.d.ts` extension) tell TypeScript about the types of variables and functions in JavaScript files, enabling type checking.

E

Enum: A special "class" that represents a group of constants (unchangeable variables). Enums allow for named sets of numeric or string values, making the code more descriptive.

F

Function Overloading: The ability to define multiple function signatures with the same name but different parameter types or numbers in TypeScript. This allows a single function to handle different data types or use cases more flexibly.

G

Generics: A feature that allows for the definition of reusable functions, classes, or interfaces that can work with any data type while providing type safety. Generics are denoted by angle brackets (e.g., ` <T> `).

I

Interface: A structure that defines the shape of an object, including its properties and methods, without implementing them. Interfaces enable strong typing and help ensure consistent object structures across a codebase.

J

JSX: JavaScript XML, a syntax extension for JavaScript commonly used with React. TypeScript supports JSX, allowing developers to write HTML-like syntax in their JavaScript code, while also benefiting from TypeScript's type-checking capabilities.

L

Literal Types: A set of specific values that a variable can hold, instead of a broader base type. Literal types can represent strings, numbers, or booleans precisely.

M

Module: A self-contained piece of code that encapsulates functionalities and exports them for use in other modules. TypeScript's module system enhances code organization and reusability.

Namespace: A way to organize and group logically related code, similar to modules, that helps avoid naming conflicts in larger applications.

O

Overriding: The ability of a subclass to provide a specific implementation of a method that is already defined in its superclass. TypeScript permits method overriding, enhancing polymorphism.

P

Promise: An object that represents the eventual completion (or failure) of an asynchronous operation and its resulting value. TypeScript allows static typing for Promises to ensure type safety.

S

Static Typing: A feature that checks types at compile time instead of at runtime. TypeScript allows developers to define types for variables, function parameters, and return values, catching errors before code execution.

Tuple: An array with a fixed number of elements, where each element can have a different type. Tuples allow developers to create arrays with heterogeneous data structures.

T

Type Annotation: A syntactical way to specify the type of a variable, function return type, or function parameter explicitly. Type annotations enhance readability and maintainability.

Type Inference: A feature where the TypeScript compiler automatically deduces the type of a variable based on its initialization. This reduces the need for explicit type annotations in many cases.

U

Union Type: A TypeScript feature that allows a variable to hold multiple types. For example, a variable can be either a string or a number, providing flexibility in handling different data forms.

V

Void: A type that indicates a function does not return a value. It is often used to define functions whose primary purpose is to perform an action rather than compute a value.

www.ingramcontent.com/pod-product-compliance
Lightning Source LLC
LaVergne TN
LVHW051335050326
832903LV00031B/3557